Genealogies of Capitalism

By the same author

LAND, LABOUR AND ECONOMIC DISCOURSE
MARXISM AND THE AGRARIAN QUESTION, two volumes
(*with Athar Hussain*)

Genealogies of Capitalism

Keith Tribe

HUMANITIES PRESS

Atlantic Highlands, New Jersey

First Published in the United States of America 1981 by
HUMANITIES PRESS INC
171 First Avenue, Atlantic Highlands, New Jersey 07716

Library of Congress Cataloging in Publication Data

Tribe, Keith.
Genealogies of capitalism.

Bibliography: p.
Includes index.
1. Economics—History. 2. Economic history.
3. Capitalism—History. 4. Agriculture—Economic aspects—English—History. I. Title.
HB75.T715 1981 330.12'2'09 80–29153
ISBN 0–391–02227–X

For Con and Harold

Contents

List of Figures

List of Tables

Preface

Despite some diversity, the essays assembled here are united by a common concern with the genesis of capitalist economic organisation. Addressing themselves to the various problems of Marxist historiography, agrarian history and the history of economic discourse, they are in fact dominated by a concern with the role that the economy plays in the writing of histories of capitalism, thus the apparent diversity of subject matter – from the Transition debate, to the agrarian structure of eighteenth century England, to the conception of 'industrialisation', to the nature of Adam Smith's economics – is structured by a constant preoccupation with the dominating categories and forms of explanation mobilised in discussions of the 'development of capitalism'. In some senses each essay takes the form of a commentary on an already-existing historical discourse, and the actual variety of problems thereby addressed dictates different forms of argument. The specific reasons for this will soon become quite clear, but it must be stated at once that there is another thread which runs through the essays, and is most clearly expressed at the end of the first: this is the realisation that the genealogy of capitalism as a genealogy of economic forms is a necessarily impossible and contradictory genealogy, in which the genealogy of a totality is sought in the constitution of economic relations, and in which the 'remaining elements' of the totality (the state, politics, the social, the ideological) are simply generated by transforming the original economic categories.

Three of the four essays are based on previously unpublished work which arose from a study of the formation of Classical Political Economy carried out during 1973 and 1974. The fourth is a revised version of an article published in 1977 which indicates in a truncated form the way in which the analysis of economic discourse was finally posed. While not wishing to overly bore the reader with personal biographical details, some indication of the circumstances in which the different pieces of work came to be undertaken might shed some light on their relation as well as tracing a sometimes painful break with the theoretical and epistemological certitudes with which the work began.

My doctoral thesis, completed at the end of 1975, was entitled *Ground Rent and the Formation of Classical Political Economy; A Theoretical History*. It sought to show how certain theoretical categories of a (narrowly defined) classical period of thought were linked to developments in economic structure – in this case, demonstrating the agrarian basis of Ricardian economic theory. By the time the thesis came to be written, an original commitment to a logico-historical account of the development of ground rent out of the genesis of capitalist agriculture into the central category of Classical Political Economy had been abandoned. Instead, three chapters of the thesis provided an outline of the structure of capitalist agriculture in eighteenth-century England which was then loosely related to the discussion of economic theory which followed. The second essay in this collection is a heavily revised version of these three chapters.

The original project of a logico-historical development of economic categories out of the economic relations which they expressed was based on a belief that Classical Political Economy was an inadequate reflection, or expression, of the economic structure of the capitalist mode of production, and represented a scientific ideology preceding the formation of a science of the economy with the work of Marx. As such the project was conceived as a historical complement to Althusser's contribution to *Reading Capital*, in which the limitations of the treatment of Marx's economics could be overcome. Gradually it became clear however that serious problems existed in Althusser's account of Marx's discoveries and innovations, which were during 1974–5 identified as originating in the distinction of science from ideology and its associated categories. During the course of a series of seminars in Cambridge organised by Terry Counihan, questions were raised concerning the manner in which Althusser introduced devices to bridge the gap that he had himself opened up between the 'real' and 'knowledge'; a gap that served the valuable service of disallowing the conception of knowledge as an abstract, ideal expression of a material, real order, but which in the final analysis did not escape the dualism which it sought to condemn. The distinction between science and ideology, differentiated according to their mode of connection to the real relations of a social order, failed to escape a collapse into the truth–falsity opposition that marked a correspondence theory of knowledge, in which the final collapse was only averted by detaching knowledge as a quasi-autonomous realm maintained by terminology such as 'scientific ideology', 'theoretical ideology', 'knowledge effect' and so on. Papers by Hindess and Hirst on these problems were particularly important in guiding discussions of the problems of Althusser's epistemology, discussions which during 1975 concluded that the arguments developed by Althusser and his associates had to be abandoned. The evaluation of Classical Political Economy in terms of epistemological criteria had therefore to be dispensed with, although this involved more than rejecting attempts to determine its ideological or scientific status. It also problematised the entire project of deducing economic categories from the process of formation of an agrarian capitalist economy.

In 1973 the general idea had been that such a deduction could be effected, tracing the formation of the capitalist mode of production and its articulation with the feudal mode of production in the transition period. The work of Balibar and Bettelheim was conceived as providing the theoretical model; it only remained to map their formulations on to historical accounts of fourteenth to seventeenth-century England. The first major problem encountered in this approach was that the most useful historical accounts for such purposes were those of Soviet historians; restricted as I was then to translations of their work, it proved impossible to carry work any further. Such a project was moreover quite unmanageable, realisable only in terms of a 'grand history' which confined itself to comfortable generalities; it is here taken up again, but in terms far removed from the project of 1973–4, seeking to show the impossibility of the terms on which it was founded.

The idea of writing an account of the genesis of the capitalist mode of production in a doctoral thesis was set on one side, and instead a more manageable treatment of the agrarian structure of the eighteenth century decided upon. Rather than deducing the categories of economic theory from the structure of capitalist relations in process of formation, this involved the more limited objective of demonstrating the relationship between Classical Political Economy and agrarian capitalism as a structure. Apart from being more realistic, it had the advantage of bearing directly on treatments of economic theory which related it to the Industrial Revolution. Classical economic theory is often treated as being a theoretical response to the rise of industrial capitalism; it is on the other hand relatively easy to show that such a conception is historically untenable, apart from the general problems involved in assigning 'real economic' developments a causal priority in the explanation of theoretical innovation. Again, work that was done on the problems of the 'Industrial Revolution' was never properly written up, and only appeared in a truncated form as part of an article entitled 'Capitalism and Industrialisation' in the Australian journal *Intervention*.

The thesis eventually emerged with two major sections: the first consisted of a description of the eighteenth-century rural economic order in England, while the second was a description of theoretical systems. The former was assigned only a general explanatory force, while the latter treated different theories as discursive ensembles in their own right. This represented a rather unsatisfactory compromise, which further reflection failed immediately to resolve; and the essay on Smith shows that the first solution was to maintain a distinction between historical and theoretical description while denying the possibility of deducing the nature of the latter from the former. This was taken further in *Land, Labour and Economic Discourse*, which through the excision of accounts of the economy as referent and 'real world' became a methodological text with a dual argument: that *general* economic categories do not exist, they are rather only formed in distinct discursive ensembles; and that the correspondence between a privileged 'economy' on the one hand and 'economic thought' on the other as a means of accounting for the shifts taking place in theoretical discourse was inadmissable. At the cost of a certain formalism, this was more or less successful, although limited by the implicit manner in which the critique of historical and epistemological accounts of economic theory was conducted.

In the last few years it has been apparent that some of the earlier work could, if suitably rewritten, bear separate publication. Here, then, are finally presented what might at first glance seem to be simply fragments of an incomplete, and uncompletable, project. There is however a difference, especially in the first essay, where the object is to demonstrate some of the reasons for the problems encountered earlier. Stated simply, the basic problem was, and here remains, that the 'economy' bears the burden of explanatory privilege in the analysis of social forms. The thread running through the different essays is that a genealogy of capitalism in terms of the economy is unworkable. The sometimes piecemeal effect of the arguments presented here is a *theoretical* effect of a refusal to artificially bind together disparate elements through an economic teleology.

But this is not to say that some more satisfactory account of the 'development of capitalism' can henceforth be written. As is hinted at the end of the first essay, part of the difficulty is that to conceive 'capitalism' as the organising principle of histories of the present is to invoke the very priority of 'economic forces' that is shown to consistently undermine the resolution of the Transition debate in a manner satisfactory to all parties involved. Insofar as Marxism is committed to such principles it must be recognised that it is committed to insoluble problems. While an 'academic Marxism' has developed rapidly over the last decade it has, paradoxically, remained trapped in the nineteenth century. To state this is in no way to capitulate to ignorant criticisms to the effect that *Capital* is 'about' nineteenth-century capitalism and thus of no relevance today. To those who suggest this it could be said that the kind of liberal economy that they envisage was a myth propagated in the early nineteenth century, although such forms of argument of course lead nowhere. More importantly it has to be realised that the domain of problems to which Marx addressed himself, and the mean which he forged for their analysis, must themselves be treated as problematic. If this is accepted, it should then become clear that the use of 'capitalism' as the most general characterisation of the contemporary complex of social, economic and political relations leads to a series of problems that must be abandoned. If academic Marxism has anything to offer at all, it must be in this area, for it at least has the facilities, if not the faculties, for the investigation of such problems.

Some attempt has been made in all the essays below to refer to recent publications where relevant, but it will be quite clear that the bulk of the material on which they are based dates from the periods indicated above. I would like to take this opportunity, somewhat belatedly, of thanking Terry Counihan and Steve Gaukroger who were largely instrumental in developing many of the arguments during 1974–5 which resulted in major changes in my own work. Since then, and during the work on these essays, further changes have taken place which are however to a great extent the systematisation of their influence. Liz Brown and Jeff Minson both gave advice and help most generously while working on this book, while Jim Tully provided friendly encouragement.

Keele, September 1979
Heidelberg, February 1980

KEITH TRIBE

Acknowledgements

The author and publishers wish to thank the following who have kindly given permission for the use of copyright material:

Cambridge University Press for a table from *British Economic Growth 1688–1959* by P. Deane and W. A. Cole;

John Wiley & Sons Ltd for some charts from 'The Turnip, The New Husbandry and the English Agricultural Revolution' by C. P. Timmer in *Quarterly Journal of Economics*, Vol. 83, 1969;

Routledge & Kegan Paul, Ltd and the editors of *Economy and Society* for permission to reprint (with slight alterations) 'The "Histories" of Economic Discourse', first published in *Economy and Society*;

the University of London Library to reproduce an extract from Laurence's *Duty of a Steward to his Lord*.

1 The Problems of Transition and the Question of Origin

The history of theoretical Marxism in Britain assumes the form of writings on history. It is a particular kind of historical writing: one which focusses on the origin and growth of capitalist relations, exploring the nature of feudalism and questions of periodisation. Debate on the nature of contemporary capitalism among Marxists has taken for granted that this is primarily a historical question – an assumption that for example made the debate between the Board of *New Left Review* and E. P. Thompson in the mid-1960s possible. As Perry Anderson wrote in 1964, 'the present crisis can, in effect, only be understood in terms of the differential formation and development of British capitalist society since the seventeenth century' (Anderson, 1964, p. 28). The burden of Thompson's criticisms were directed against the manner in which historical arguments were then deployed, while the overall strategy was never questioned. Anderson has since gone on to push the boundaries of historical research a few centuries further back, while Thompson has concentrated on the structure of relations in eighteenth-century England.

A concern for the origins of capitalist forms as a means of analysing the nature of British capitalist development had of course been classically represented by the so-called 'Transition debate' of the 1940s and early 1950s, and the re-publication of some of these orginal contributions by New Left Books in 1976 indicated the continuing interest in the issues that had been raised. During the previous year however a book had been published which appeared to forcefully reject the project of a genealogy of capitalism as a central means of contemporary analysis – Hindess and Hirst's *Pre-Capitalist Modes of Production.* Examining in turn the various candidates presented by Marx for historical periodisation, these were treated not as entities to be assessed through historical argument, but rather as theoretical objects. Taking as a point of departure problems raised by Balibar in his contribution to *Reading Capital*, they sought to either construct a general concept for each mode of production or show that such a general concept could not be produced (Hindess and Hirst, 1975, p. 1). While devoting a great deal of space to the much-discussed nature of the feudal mode of production and the nature of the transition to capitalism, the dismissal of 'the notion of history as a coherent and worthwhile object of study' (p. 321) appeared to mark a break with the traditions of British Marxism. This 'rejection of history' is in fact extremely ambiguous, since by virtue of their concentration on non-capitalist modes of production (although not endowed with historical time) Hindess and Hirst in many ways simply continued the established historico-theoretical practices of British Marxism, while apparently developing an alternative.

If the roll of prominent British Marxist historians is called – and among them would number Dobb, Hill, Hobsbawm, Hilton, Thompson and Morton – at least two planes emerge to link them. Firstly, the credentials of their Marxism are established in their pre-eminent concern with economic relations in the periods that they study. Secondly, these periods lie in the main before the mid-nineteenth century. Classical British Marxism is then not only historical, but weighted towards analyses of economic forces (and the social forces thereby engendered) in Britain before 1850.

We can however isolate a more exact date: 1867, the year of publication of *Capital* Volume 1. For what goes on in such historical writings is the reworking of the genesis of capitalist forms that Marx offered in his analysis of the capitalist mode of production. Dobb's *Studies in the Development of Capitalism* can be regarded for example as a systematisation of the genealogical elements deployed by Marx, while Thompson's *Making of the English Working Class* conforms to the periodisation of the English labour movement outlined in *Capital.* In such historical writings adherence to, or deviation from, Marxist doctrine could be easily established simply by reference to indications supplied by Marx personally. This possibility, opened up by Marx's use of the English case as the classical form of capitalist development, lent historical writing a particular rigour while at the same time inhibiting its development.

Capital is not of course a work of history in the modern sense, although Marx described it as a 'natural history'; it rather seeks to develop the principal characteristics of the capitalist mode of production in a logico-historical fashion. The various elements of capitalist production are first identified and then ascribed a process of historical development; this can be seen for example in Volume 1, Chapters 13 and 14, where the formation of factory production is shown to follow on from manufacture in the development of forms of the division of labour. The most sustained historical passages in this volume are to be found in the final part, under the title 'So-Called Primitive Accumulation'. This is described as nothing more than the historical process of separation of the producer from the means of production, 'primitive' in form because this concerns the pre-history of capital and its corresponding mode of production. The foundation of this whole process of separation is the expropriation of rural producers, beginning in England in the late fifteenth century, which within two centuries had resulted in the creation of a landless proletariat on the one hand and a class of capitalist farmers on the other. This agricultural revolution in turn laid the basis for the development of a home market for industrial capital, and in combination with the transformation of other sections of capital the basis was laid for the industrial and commercial development of capitalism. Coming as it does in the final pages of the book, this treatment of the historical origins of capitalism assumes the status of a reprise, rather than of a point of departure.

In the analysis of rent which can be found in Volume 3, however, there is an investigation of the early forms of surplus extraction in the form of rent which is more directly linked to the theoretical narrative. Here can be found first a critique of early economists and their naturalisation of the source of rent, and then a differentiation of forms of pre-capitalist rent. Labour rent, product rent and money rent are described as variant means for the extraction of surplus labour, whose function from the point of view of the capitalist mode of production is to effect the expropriation of possessors from the land with the introduction of money rent, at first the most developed form of its predecessors. With this last form the conditions are created for the appearance of capitalist tenant farmers, either out of the ranks of prosperous peasants or *via* the entry into agricultural production of capital accumulated elsewhere. These historical forms of rent are consequently geared to an explanation of the manner in which capitalist relations took root and developed out of forms that were themselves non-capitalist. Balibar has emphasised that this analysis of primitive accumulation must be regarded as a genealogy which, element by element, far from projecting back the structure of capitalist relations, is structured according to a knowledge of a 'historical outcome'. At its most fundamental, this genealogy accounts for the formation of two main elements entering into the capitalist structure – the 'free' labourer (written as the history of the separation of the producer from the means of production) and capital (the history of usury and merchant capital). The analysis of primitive accumulation is thus quite distinct from the history of previous modes of production (Balibar, 1970, pp. 279–80).

Capital is primarily then an analysis of the capitalist mode of production, conceived as a specific form of economy, in which historical descriptions of other economic forms enter only insofar as they illuminate aspects of the origin and development of this mode of production. Some of this historical description is polemical, directed against those who sought to identify capitalist production with all but the most primitive forms of human organisation. Some of it is necessary for the identification of distinct phases of capitalist evolution. In either case, the role of history is circumscribed by its function as genealogy.

Marx also proposes that while his argument is restricted to an analysis of economic relations, this does at the same time make possible an examination of political and social forms which are held to correspond to these economic relations. Consider this well-known passage, from the section of Volume 3, Chapter 48 which deals with labour rent:

> The specific economic form, in which unpaid surplus-labour is pumped out of direct producers, determines the relationship of rulers and ruled, as it grows directly out of production itself and, in turn, reacts upon it as a determining element. Upon this, however, is founded the entire formation of the

> economic community which grows up out of the production relations themselves, thereby its specific political form. It is always the direct relationship of the owner of the conditions of production to the direct producers – a relation always naturally corresponding to a definite stage in the development of the methods of labour and thereby its social productivity – which reveals the innermost secret, the hidden basis of the entire social structure, and with it the political form of the relation of sovereignty and dependence, in short, the corresponding specific form of the state. (*Capital,* Vol. 3, p.791)

Economic relations between producers and exploiters of surplus labour are thus the 'secret life' of society, determining the form of political relations and ultimately the nature of the state. *Capital* presents no analysis of the political forms corresponding to the capitalist mode of production, but it is suggested, here and in other passages, that once the economic relations are uncovered then the discovery of the real nature of political forces is achieved. The history of capital that Marx writes is thus not only a genealogy, but a genealogy of economic forms – in modern terms, economic history.

This is reflected in the writings of classical Marxist historical scholarship in Britain; deviations from the tradition can furthermore be accounted for as deviations from Marxism. Thus the developing concern of Christopher Hill since the 1950s with religion and politics in the seventeenth century can be regarded as a steady departure from principles of orthodox Marxism expressed in his earlier writings. Similarly E. P. Thompson's work on the eighteenth century in its socio-cultural concerns also tacitly departs from the imperatives outlined by Marx. Many would argue that such departures were 'creative', but the issue that is of concern here is not the checking of credentials and revocation of licences to practise. Such a critical stance would imply complicity with the tradition of Marxist history that is here being examined, re-establishing a pantheon *via* the application of 'Marxist principles', or indeed a comparison with the word of Marx on a number of historical issues. Marxist historical writing in Britain takes the form in the main of an elaboration on themes established by Marx in *Capital*. The question that arises from this concerns the effects that this has on the function and writing of Marxist history in Britain. In order to assess such effects it is necessary to consider more closely the writings of Marxist historians, and so there is presented below a discussion of the so-called 'Transition debate'. The purpose of this presentation is the elaboration of certain aspects of Marxist historiography out of a classical source; it is not of course presumed that this exhausts the concerns of Marxist writing, merely that it concisely illuminates general problems of Marxist analysis. This will be demonstrated later on, when the problematic features of the Transition debate are related to the more recent contributions of Anderson and Brenner.

It is commonly assumed that the debate over the transition from feudalism to capitalism was conducted mainly in the pages of *Science and Society* following Sweezy's review in 1950 of Dobb's *Studies in the Development of Capitalism* (1946). The contributions to this debate were reprinted in a separate booklet by the publishers of *Science and Society* in 1954, and then this booklet, together with more recent related papers, was re-published by New Left Books in 1976. Rodney Hilton provided an introduction to this last edition which both provided a background to the debate and outlined some of the results of more recent research on the nature of the feudal economy and its dissolution.

While he was a participant in this debate, the introduction that Hilton provides is very misleading for modern readers. A casual perusal of the relevant copies of *Science and Society* for the later 1940s would immediately reveal that the issues involved in this debate have a somewhat longer history than Hilton is prepared to allow. Hill for example had published two articles on the English Civil War and its historical interpretations in 1948, and in his 'Historians on the Rise of British Capitalism' (which was published later in the same year as Sweezy's review of Dobb) there is reference to an extensive literature on the politics and economics of the transition that Hilton never refers to (Hill, 1950). In fact, strictly speaking, the Transition debate began in 1940, with the publication of Hill's *The English Revolution 1640* – and Hill's interpretation of the economic basis of this revolution rested heavily on foundations established by Soviet historians in the 1920s and 1930s. Kosminsky in a survey of 1928 had emphasised the well-established interest of Russian scholars stimulated by the manner in which Marx and Engels had relied on the 'English model' of capitalist development, beginning with the work of Kovalevsky, and including Granat's *The Disapperance of the Peasantry in England* (1908) which explicitly took issue with Marx's account of expropriation in the sixteenth century (Kosminsky, 1928, p. 222). Kosminsky's *English Village in the Thirteenth Century* (1935) was known to English historians through Postan's review in the *Economic History Review* (1936), and Hill himself had published a survey of Soviet studies of the Interregnum in 1938. Hill's extensive acquaintance with Soviet historical research in the later 1930s was again demonstrated in his 'Agrarian Legislation of the Interregnum' (1940b), which summarised Arkhangelsky's work on this subject. *The English Revolution 1640* can be seen in part as the outcome of a study of Soviet research into feudalism and its dissolution, in which of course questions of Marxist theory and adherence to Marxist doctrine were a major preoccupation. As will be seen, the Transition debate concerned mainly problems of economics and politics in Marxist analysis, and only with Sweezy's comparatively late intervention did it become restricted to one of the economics of transition. To confine attention to what were in fact the closing stages of a lengthy debate, as Hilton does, diverts attention from some of the central problems that the discussions encountered.

In his contribution to *The English Revolution 1640* Hill was concerned to demonstrate that the English Civil War was a class war, destroying an essentially feudal order and paving the way for capitalist development. The crumbling of a stable and feudal order, 'made up of isolated local communities producing for their own consumption, with very little trade between them' (Hill, 1940a, p. 22), began in the fifteenth century with the development of trade in food and wool, which resulted in the gradual transformation of producers into commodity producers in a national market. Land itself became a commodity, and the marketing of the produce from land so regarded led to the treatment of rents as a source of profit linked to commodity production. There followed a period of the progressive 'racking-up' of rents which was as much a moral as an economic revolution, destroying conceptions of custom and tradition (pp. 22–3). Trade and manufacturing showed similar tendencies, outstripping the limitations of the forms in which they were contained.

England in 1640 was economically a feudal state, argued Hill, but with a capitalist sector that could not forever be kept in check. The class forces engendered by this economic balance were described as follows:

> There were really three classes in conflict. As against the parasitic feudal landowners and speculative financiers, the interests of the new class of capitalist merchants and farmers were temporarily identical with those of the small peasantry and artisans and journeymen. But conflict between the two latter classes was bound to develop, since the expansion of capitalism involved the dissolution of the old agrarian and industrial relationships and the transformation of independent small masters and peasants into proletarians. (pp. 36–7)

In this situation the Tudor state held the balance between the bourgeoisie and the progressive gentry on the one hand, and the 'feudalists' on the other; but by the end of the sixteenth century, the bourgeoisie ceased to need the protection of the monarchy, and the monarchy in turn was becoming aware of the growing power of the bourgeoisie. The early seventeenth century saw a series of clashes between the Crown and nascent capitalists, the tempo of struggle rising to a climax with the outbreak of a Civil War which was at its inception a clash between a monarchy wedded to feudal privilege and a progressive bourgeoisie.

The main lines of Hill's essay are clear, and the purpose here is not to become involved in an evaluation of the evidence that he advances in support of an admittedly schematic account of a complex period. The principal significance of Hill's essay is that it gave rise to a debate in the pages of *Labour Monthly*, which was followed by a lengthy discussion among Communist historians. As we shall see, this discussion resulted in the publication in 1946 of Dobb's *Studies in the Development of Capitalism*, and in a series of articles in *Communist Review* and *Modern Quarterly*, both publications of the Communist Party of Great Britain. Partly this was a result of the fact that the decade of the 1940s presented historians with a succession of tercentenaries of major events of the Civil War, each of which could be celebrated with a publication. But more seriously than this, the manner in which the Civil War was discussed in these now-neglected pieces (which of course would be cursorily dismissed by any modern historian of the period) illuminates in a very direct way the manner in which British Marxism 'thinks historically'.

Hill's book was reviewed in *Labour Monthly* in October 1940 by a critic going under the cryptic signature of 'P.F.', but who was in fact Jürgen Kuczynski. Disagreement was immediately registered with Hill's interpretation of the political and economic conditions leading up to the Civil War; the periodisation of feudalism and capitalism that was offered was described as 'not new but it contradicts that which Marx and Engels and other students of English history have given' (Kuczynski, 1940a, p. 558). Marx, Kuczynski argued, had defined sixteenth-century England as 'definitely bourgeois, that is, capitalist' and cited a letter written to Engels in 1858 to this effect (*Selected Correspondence,* p. 117). Thus if the sixteenth century was already fundamentally the period of capitalist consolidation in England, Hill's explanation of the class character of the Civil War is in error. This is spelled out by Kuczynski as follows:

> But Marx rightly points out that it was not feudal, it was bourgeois, and, therefore, the demands of the capitalists are executed and encouraged by the monarchs, who are also capitalists.
>
> Elizabeth was not a feudal monarch bowing to the demands of an oppressed capitalist class. She was the most prominent capitalist in capitalist bourgeois society . . . (1940a, p. 559)

In this version then, supported by some comments of Marx and Engels, the Civil War becomes the response by the bourgeoisie to a counter-revolution led by the monarchists which has as its object the maintenance, rather than the establishment, of bourgeois political power. The above characterisation of class forces might appear today as naive and dogmatic, but it does betray a theoretical approach which is common to more modern and apparently sophisticated 'neo-Marxian' histories, such as Wallerstein's *Modern World System* for instance. The parallels will be elaborated later, but attention must be drawn at this point to the equivocal terminology used by Kuczynski to describe class forces. In some places 'bourgeois' and 'capitalist' are used interchangeably, in others the slide from one to the other marks a slight unease. It will be noticed that this equivocation is endemic to the transition controversy, and in fact signifies one of its central contradictions, namely the problem of the relation between political and economic forces in social formations.

In December 1940 *Labour Monthly* printed a reply to Kuczynski by Douglas Garman, followed by a response from Kuczynski. Garman suggested that Hill had been misread, but did so in a manner which effectively allowed the points originally made. The principal objection that Garman made was that if Kuczynski were right in his periodisation of state and class in England, then the logical result of such propositions was reformism (Garman, 1940, p. 653). While familiar, such arguments were hardly decisive, and Kuczynski replied by reiterating his original remarks. He did however elaborate on the nature of political rule in the sixteenth century, and introduced the idea that the Tudor monarchy was in fact absolutist, ruling in the interests of the bourgeoisie, but by the mid-seventeenth century a fetter on the further development of capitalist enterprise.

> Absolute monarchy was a product of bourgeois development in England at a time when this form of government and its institutions were a valuable safeguard against feudalism. With the progress of capitalism, absolute monarchy became a hindrance. . . . [The Civil War was thus] a fight for the abolition of the absolute monarchy, against the remnants of feudalism, against the reactionary sections of the bourgeoisie, against every element which might retard the vigorous development of bourgeois capitalist society. (Kuczynski 1940b, p. 654)

This conception of absolute monarchy differs only in periodisation from that of Hill, who likewise saw the Tudor state as a device holding a balance of economic and political forces in equilibrium while permitting capitalist expansion. The question of periodisation however conceals a deeper problem, and this was first isolated by Dona Torr in a contribution published in February 1941.

Kuczynski's most serious mistake, she suggested, was his assumption ('specifically refuted by Marx and Lenin') that self-sufficient manorial economy passed straight into capitalist economy:

> Ignoring the intermediate stages of small commodity production, essential to capitalist development, he omits from his

> survey of sixteenth century English society the largest section, the peasantry, and uses the categories of a later stage, assuming that the existence of a considerable number of proletarians implies the establishment of capitalist society.
>
> (Torr, 1941, p. 90)

This results, argues Torr, in a transition which postulates the appearance of advanced forms of capitalist relations out of the decline of feudalism. It can indeed be seen from the account given above that there are some curious features of Kuczyinski's argument: the 'absolutist state' is treated now as a transitional state form, now as a fully capitalist form, while capitalist relations of production themselves are in no need of historical modification, since they arrive fully developed at their moment of emergence.

Torr suggests that when Kuczynski calls sixteenth-century agriculture 'essentially capitalist' he fails to consider the problem of combination of diverse economic forms. If this were taken into account, it would be clear that capitalist agriculture was not the 'dominant mode of production' in the sixteenth century. In posing the problem in this fashion, Torr opened the way for an extended debate on the issues raised by Hill and Kuczynski which would make possible the examination of theoretical propositions concerning the transition between distinct socio-political orders. The form this examination would take was however primarily in terms of arguments on the development of British capitalism; but the significance of the problems raised went beyond this limitation.

Other errors committed by Kuczynski were identified by Torr, such as a confusion of the stage of manufacture with that of factory production, a confusion which is attributable to the conception of capitalist relations as unchanging entities. But more importantly, attention was drawn to the manner in which Kuczynski argued that if capitalism was dominant, then bourgeois society must also exist – that is, social and political forces were simply deduced from, and assumed to co-exist with, appropriate economic forces. This misconception is corrected with the aid of a quotation from the 1859 'Preface' and one from *Anti-Duhring*, which are deployed in order to establish that orthodox Marxism emphasised the dialectical disjunction between economic, social and political change. However, the role of dialectics in this case seems merely that it supplies a time-lag which enables

Torr to escape from the 'big-bang' theory of social revolution while retaining the derivation of political forces from economic forces.

Torr's allegiance to the basic principles that are most starkly presented by Kuczynski is apparent in the criticisms that are made of the original characterisation of Queen Elizabeth as a capitalist; Torr points out that the trade monopolies of the Tudor and Stuart Crown were not personal, but an 'integral part of feudal-absolutist State power' (p. 91). This 'feudal-absolutist' state appears to combine the positions of both Torr and Kuczynski in the mode of identification of the state form characteristic of the period of transition that Torr had argued for. The distance from Kuczynski's version of the Tudor monarchy is established by Torr in her suggestion that the former, in his second formulation of the relation of capitalists to the absolutist state, simply repeated the mistake of Pokrovsky. It was perhaps unfortunate that Kuczynski had relied on the wrong edition of the *Great Soviet Encyclopedia* (in which Pokrovsky had contributed an account of the development of capitalism in England), but Torr could not produce a more satisfactory and coherent description of the nature of the Tudor state than that she was criticising.

Following the contribution of Dona Torr there comes one from Maurice Dobb who, in contrast to Garman and Torr, accepts the central point made by Kuczynski while objecting to the latter's failure to either recognise the merits of Hill's essay as a first attempt at an understanding of the seventeenth-century revolution, or provide a more positive clue to an alternative interpretation. The real weakness of Hill's essay is perceived by Dobb to lie in the way in which it glosses over important changes in the mode of production which present problems for Marxists. These problems are outlined as follows:

> If one dates the rise of capitalism as a mode of production from the industrial revolution of the eighteenth century (as is sometimes done), then Marxists are confronted with this problem. How could the seventeenth-century struggle be treated as a bourgeois-democratic revolution when it came a century and a half before the rise of capitalist production? Whence a bourgeoisie to carry through the revolution, if the capitalist mode of production was not yet in being at all?

> Moreover, what *was* the prevailing mode of production in Stuart England anyhow? (Dobb, 1941, p. 92)

Kuczynski, Dobb argued, was correct when he denied that the feudal mode of production was dominant in Stuart England. But to identify this epoch as one of merchant capitalism was evasive, since this form did not penetrate into production until later in the development of capitalism. Dobb proceeds to outline the transition from feudalism to capitalism in terms of a disjunction between the relations and forces of production prevailing in the later fifteenth century, to be followed by a gradual transformation of handicraft industry into capitalist manufacture in the early sixteenth century. This also had affected the development of agriculture and textiles. As these forces developed they gradually came into conflict with merchant capitalists who had entered into an alliance with feudal remnants in order to preserve their privileges: 'whence the seventeenth-century revolution' concludes Dobb (p. 93).

Thus the first contributions to the 'Transition debate', as it was later to be known, were concluded. The original argument over the nature of the revolution that took place in the seventeenth century had been substantially refined in terms of the conceptualisation of economic relations, while the problem of the political forms arising on these relations was if anything more confused. It was assumed by all the contributors of course that to specify the problem in this manner was authorised by Marx and consequently itself unproblematic. A more exact specification of the sixteenth and seventeenth-century English economy appeared to be the most pressing analytical problem, and in the year following the war Maurice Dobb published a book which dealt with this in detail – *Studies in the Development of Capitalism.* But it must be noted at this point that the contributors to *Labour Monthly* had displayed some confusion in the typology of political forms that was not directly related to the absence of consensus on the economic structure, and as will be shown the publication of a work which made possible such a consensus simply revivified this confusion.

The overall project of *Studies* was to illuminate the nature of contemporary capitalism through an examination of aspects of its genesis, and in this respect the book reads in places very much as an exegesis of the historical sections and passages to be found in *Capital*. Capitalism was treated as an historical entity, whose specificity in time and space had to be identified – for if capitalism did not exist or was synonymous with human production, then those who sought to overthrow it were struggling in vain, and Marx would be discredited (Dobb, 1963, p. 2). Accordingly the first chapter of the book deals with various definitions of capitalism before going on to elaborate Marx's emphasis on commodity production as the defining characteristic of the capitalist mode of production. The inception of capitalism is however distinguished from the simple appearance of commodity relations in the economy; also critical are the class relationships which these relations give rise to, and in outlining this relation between economic and political structure Dobb reiterates the position taken by Marx in the citation from Volume 3 above. Consequently the first period of capitalist expansion is not to be found in the emergence of merchants and traders, but rather in the political and social transformations of the seventeenth century (p. 18).

It might be noted that this declaration places the emergence of capitalism rather later than in the *Labour Monthly* piece, and also has as an effect the denial of a possibility of the 'decline of feudalism' being attributable to the 'rise of capitalism'. The crisis of feudalism begins for Dobb in the fourteenth and fifteenth centuries, while the development of capitalism can be dated really only from the early seventeenth century. Between these two orders lies a system that is 'neither feudal nor yet capitalist so far as its mode of production is concerned' (p. 19).

> It is also true, and of outstanding importance for any proper understanding of this transition, that the disintegration of the feudal mode of production had already reached an advanced stage *before* the capitalist mode of production developed, and that this disintegration did not proceed in any close association with the growth of the new mode of production within the womb of the old. (Dobb, 1963, p. 20)

This position thus opens up a period of two hundred years within which no mode of production can be said to be dominant, but rather there takes place a process of transition to capitalism. This conclusion rests chiefly on a rejection of those who treat a merchant bourgeoisie as 'capitalists' in a modern sense, and also those arguments which deal with the problem of the transition from feudalism to capitalism through the application of historical teleology: the identification of the dissolution of feudalism with the necessary rise of capitalism, a view which Marx was well-known for. As we shall see, in opening up this space and refusing to write a history in this manner Dobb makes a serious attempt to pose problems in the politics and economics of transition periods. A problem does however persist in that by the very description of such a period as 'transitional' the problems of genealogy are not necessarily avoided.

While the second chapter of *Studies* in entitled 'The Decline of Feudalism and the Growth of Towns' these two factors are not directly linked. In fact the bulk of the chapter concerns the structure of the English feudal economy and the reason for its demise, and only after this has been dealt with are towns discussed at any length. For Dobb, feudalism is associated with the existence of serfdom, since it is identified by a particular form of extraction of surplus labour from direct producers. Feudalism was not the same as 'natural economy'; serfdom was not equivalent to the extraction of surplus labour only in the form of labour services, for this relation could be monetised without altering its basic economic form. Dobb argued then that serfdom could be expressed by a number of economic relations (as had been outlined by Marx), and that furthermore the dissolution of a feudal economy could not be traced to the appearance of monetary relations or the commutation of labour services. Money and trade were thus ruled out as explanatory factors in the demise of feudalism.

Indeed, Dobb rejects such arguments so strongly that he is led to postulate that the eventual collapse of the various forms of feudal economy was the outcome of an internal contradiction: the inefficiency of feudalism as a system of production faced with the rising demands of lords for revenue (p. 42). A number of features of the medieval economy ensured that production remained at a feeble level, whether secular or ecclesiastical landlords' demesnes were considered, or those lands of villeins and freemen. In times of particularly heavy pressure the demands of the landlord simply destroyed the labour-base on which he rested – an argument that might today be recognised as one relatively close to the 'demographic' explanation of the medieval economy advanced by Postan.

The chronology of the collapse that is put forward is derivative of both economic and legal changes. It is proposed that by the end of the fifteenth century 'the feudal order had disintegrated and grown weaker in a number of ways' (p. 65). The old nobility had lost their former power, smaller estates had taken to leasing or to wage-labour 'as soon as the increase of population and in particular of the ranks of the poorer peasantry had made labour cheap again' (p. 65). Merchants were buying into agricultural land and estates were at the same time being mortgaged, peasant producers were becoming involved in both labour and product markets. The final disintegration of the feudal mode of production did not however come in the sixteenth century as a result of its economic collapse: Dobb argues that it was not until the Civil War that the end came. Personal bonded service and its obligations survived in some areas until the end of the sixteenth century, and feudal tenures were not abolished until 1646. Tawney pointed out in his review of *Studies* that to place such emphasis on the legal dismantling of feudal relations resulted in a very misleading picture (Tawney, 1978, p. 206). It can be suggested however that this over-emphasis on legal relations on the part of Dobb was dictated by a necessity to demonstrate the existence of substantial feudal remnants on the eve of the Civil War, providing the demise of feudalism with a chronology that comfortably spanned the period of transition.

A similar problem emerges in the later passages where Dobb seeks to identify the sources of capital accumulation that preceded the development of capitalism in the seventeenth century. In some respects Dobb here falls foul of the 'gentry' controversy, but the substance of such arguments is here less important than the function which they fulfil. The problem arises because in *Studies* the development of capitalism is not accounted for simply as the genesis of industrial production, but instead the importance of agrarian capitalist development is quite rightly emphasised. Partly this is accounted for in the emergence of a peasant bourgeoisie, but the existence of improving landlords and tenant farmers was clearly the principal form in which capitalist agriculture developed. In this process then it is necessary to account for capitalist oriented landlords and the gradual interpenetration of landed and industrial capital.

The chapter on capital accumulation accordingly begins by posing a number of alternative scenarios for the increase of landed property in bourgeois hands. Two main possibilities are isolated: purchase from former owners in exchange for means of immediate consumption, combined with windfall gains, profit inflation and swollen urban rents; or the acquisition by the bourgeoisie of property cheaply or even free, later realised at a higher price for things with a lower valuation. If this latter possibility could be confirmed, it would also account for the 'gap' isolated at the beginning of the book between the demise of feudalism and the rise of capitalism.

> If this disintegration itself had to be the historical lever for launching the process of capital accumulation, then the growth of capitalist production could not itself provide the chief agency for that disintegration. An interval had to elapse during which the petty mode of production, which was the legacy of feudal society, was itself being partially broken up or else subordinated to capital, and State policy was being shaped by new bourgeois influences in a direction favourable to bourgeois aims. (Dobb, 1963, p. 181)

Thus a transfer of lands into bourgeois hands becomes a major element in the explanation of the chronology of transition. Two factors are identified. Firstly, the economic distress of large feudal owners and small landowners in the early sixteenth century 'must have' facilitated easy purchase on the part of a parvenu bourgeoisie, in combination with new debt instruments which made foreclosure more simple. Secondly, the price inflation of the sixteenth century 'was no doubt' a powerful factor in the transfer of land into bourgeois hands.

Thus the transfer of lands into bourgeois hands is accounted for by what is in effect speculative reasoning, the speculation being founded of course in teleology. No less important however is that the *reversal* of this process has to be discovered in the later seventeenth and early eighteenth centuries, 'the objects of the original accumulation [being] realised or sold (at least in part) in order to make possible an actual investment in industrial production' (Dobb, 1963, p. 182). The conditions for such a reversal would be factors such as a firm market in land, elastic and cheap labour supply, and the availability of raw materials and production facilities.

Having established a mechanism for the genesis of industrial capital which also accounts for the length of the transition period, the pages following this set of arguments recount examples which confirm this basic analysis. The relation between 'theory' and 'history' here is however an uneasy one, where the argument first establishes that certain events must have happened if a certain outcome is observed, and then historical cases are marshalled as confirmation for theoretical hypotheses. While recognising that the organisation of a narrative should not be confused with the form in which historical generalisations are arrived at, the status of *Studies* as a historical work can on the evidence of such passages be called into question.

This is not however a criticism – rather it is necessary to point out that as a historical account of capitalist development it is dominated by the presence of a Marxist account of capitalist relations which subordinates and organises the problems that are to be analysed. The continual presence of these demands renders the book defective from the point of view of an economic historian such as Tawney, but the preservation of Marxist principles dictates that this should be so. In fact the value of *Studies* depends on its ambiguous status as a work of historical analysis, since it never departs from its project of accounting for the contemporary structure of capitalist relations through study of their genesis. If the book were more satisfactory as a work of economic history, it can be suggested that its contribution to the analysis of capitalism would (in Marxist terms) be diminished.

Emile Burns' review of *Studies*, interestingly entitled 'The Story of Capitalism', concentrated on providing a summary of the main conclusions of the book, in so doing placing the text back firmly in the arguments among Party historians over the rise of capitalism and the bourgeois revolution. During the later 1940s a series of articles appeared in *Communist Review* which developed such themes; and what became very clear was the manner in which assessment of Soviet history was played out through discussion of the transition from feudalism to capitalism. Perhaps most significant here is the publication in 1948 of a report of discussion among Party historians under the title 'State and Revolution in Tudor and Stuart England', which took up many of the problems first raised in the *Labour Monthly* discussions in the light of Dobb's *Studies in the Development of Capitalism*.

The report in *Communist Review* omits the names of the participants, but among them were Christopher Hill, Maurice Dobb, Victor Kiernan, Rodney Hilton, Brian Pearce, Dona Torr and Eric Hobsbawm. The minutes of the meetings concerned show further that the major argument took place over the question of absolutism and its relation to the economy, in which the group was reconstituted as Star Chamber with Hill in the role of executioner. Since this discussion involved some of the most prominent British Marxist historians of the 1950s and 1960s, and because the central disagreement is so significant, a summary of the discussion usefully illuminates several of the points made above. The article is dealt with first, and then followed with material drawn from the minutes of the meetings concerned.

The two general questions facing contributors are described in *Communist Review* as: firstly, how are the determining class relations of a given society identified?; and secondly, what is a social revolution?

> The first question arose in the concrete form: What were the predominant relations of men in production in England at the beginning of the seventeenth century? Was it a feudal or bourgeois society? Some of the points of method which emerged in thrashing out this question are also relevant to the question: what is a capitalist and what is a Socialist society? – where clarity is so greatly needed today.
>
> The second question arose in the concrete form: what class controlled the State between the accession of the Tudors in 1485 (or of the Yorkists in 1461) and 1640? Did the State serve the bourgeoisie and combat feudalism, or not? The underlying questions of how we determine the class character of a given State and what is the role of the State in the transition from one social order to another are very topical indeed. (Historians' Group, 1948b, pp. 208–9)

The role of the past in discussing the present is of course sharply brought out here – and in fact the article concludes with the assertion that an understanding of contemporary Eastern Europe is improved by an understanding of 1649. But it is the more specific problems of class, economy and politics which direct the ensuing account. As can be seen, these problems are conceived in broadly the same way as Kuczynski and Torr present them, and the disagreement which arose on these topics also revived some of the original criticisms.

Hill's description of early seventeenth-century England as 'feudal' is upheld in the report, emphasis being given to the relations of landlords and direct producers and the form of extraction of surplus labour; although it is conceded that power had been modified through its centralisation during the sixteenth century. The doubt arising over the feudal nature of English society in 1600 was attributed to a mistaken allegiance to view, propagated by Pokrovsky, that an epoch of 'merchant capitalism' lay between feudalism on the one hand and capitalism on the other (Historians' Group, 1948b, p.210). Instead, it is argued, this space is occupied by a period of transition, whose levels of development can be measured in the degree of separation of the producer from his means of production. In the sixteenth and seventeenth centuries, the 'decisive labour force' retained control of their means of production and the mobility of labour was inhibited. Consideration of the role of merchants and craftsmen show that economic relations were only partially capitalist, their effective development blocked by the state, controlled by feudal elements. Political forces, the implication is, blocked economic forces, and revolutionary change was required to permit the development of capitalism.

This raised the problem of the nature of the state. This is described initially as 'absolutist', a centralised feudal executive in which the results of such centralisation were favourable to capitalists. Again, the broad outlines of Hill's original essay are adhered to, and it is suggested that it is only after the period 1640–49 that it is possible to speak of a state subordinated to capitalist interests. Feudal-absolute monarchy gave way to constitutional monarchy, and the state was at the service of a new landlord–capitalist alliance (Historians' Group, 1948b, p. 213).

The report concludes by noting that in the discussions two main trends of non-Marxist thought 'revealed themselves'. The first was economic determinism, which ascribed to politics the role of adjusting itself to economics, identified therefore state with society and consequently held an evolutionary and reformist perspective. The other trend failed to ascribe to economics a determining role at all. The first forgot dialectics, the second materialism:

> The change from one mode of production to another, involving the substitution of one predominant type of production

> relations for another, takes place through class struggle, in which the exploiting class of the old order fights hard with all the means at its command (including State power) to retard the change and retain economic ascendancy.
>
> (Historians' Group, 1948b, p.214)

This assertion of the 'true Marxist' position against deviants is however marked by a certain lack of theoretical honesty. Is it fair after all to dub a view as non-Marxist because politics is ascribed a position from which it automatically adjusts to economics, while asserting a 'Marxist' position which does the same? After all, the difference can be reduced simply to one of time (history), for there is no doubt in the citation above that politics is fighting a losing battle against economics. In fact, the 'two principal errors' that arose in the discussions are really one, united in the person of Victor Kiernan, who questioned the characterisation of the seventeenth-century state as 'absolutist'.

Pokrovsky had not only suggested that there was a transitional mode of production in the existence of merchant capital, but he had also indicated that absolutism was a form of state power corresponding to this mode of production. Hill had in late 1947 prepared some 'Theses on Absolutism in England' in which the view was expressed that the Tudor state was a feudal-absolutist landowners' state. Kiernan dissented from this, arguing that Tudor revenues were not essentially feudal, nor were those of landlords; feudal tenures at this time were nominal, and he went on to suggest that it was absurd to define feudalism in such a fashion that it covered everything from primitive communism to developed capitalism. Merchant capitalism was he felt 'a good category' for filling in part of the gaps that existed; and Dobb, summing up, agreed that a better appreciation of the different types of feudal structure was necessary.

He also suggested that a committee might be formed to examine the matter, but instead of this a different means was employed for the settling of disputes: Kiernan was forced at a meeting in January to withdraw his main contentions after criticism led by Hill. Kiernan's argument that the Tudor state was absolutist, but not feudal, was allied to his argument that rather than there taking place one bourgeois revolution, there had in fact been a series – and both politics and history demanded that such arguments be rejected. Hill did so in the strongest terms:

> This controversy is of great political importance, because the Bourgeois revolution is still a real political issue in Asia, South East Europe, Spain and other parts of the world. Pokrovsky, by ante-dating the Bourgeois Revolution, in fact played into the hands of Trotskyism. His view leads to underrating the role of the State, to the assumption that bourgeios politics always reflects economic development and thus to a denial of the role of the party and of leadership. Pokrovskyism is fundamentally reformist because it assumes that a transfer of power is possible without revolution, or at least it has a blurred idea of what a revolution is, conceiving the bourgeoisie as somehow obtaining a share of power without ousting the feudal ruling class. (Historians' Group, 1948a, p. 4)

In this way the basic periodisation established in 1940 was maintained, despite the clear theoretical shortcoming that it presented. The 'gap' opened by Dobb in economic development was closed at the level of political forms by arguments that whatever mediations there were, the state confronting progressive forces in 1640 was basically feudal. In some ways this can be seen as a desperate attempt to create a large and plausibly reactionary obstacle to capitalist forces, and the problems that this created in terms of rewriting history was one of the points that had engendered Kiernan's criticisms. In denying that the analysis of the Civil War could be treated in such a mechanical and simplistic fashion he admitted that the bourgeois elements of Tudor England had been exaggerated.

But Kiernan's dilemma is clear enough: if the sixteenth century is neither feudal nor capitalist (as Dobb had in any case already implied), what state form corresponds to this? The formula 'feudal-absolutist' is deeply contradictory, as Kiernan quite rightly noted; for the point about feudal political organisation is that is is *dispersed*, and to suggest that centralisation is merely a 'final phase' is inaccurate. The formula 'feudal-absolutist' does service principally as a means of recognising the centralising tendencies in politics during the sixteenth century while ascribing the effects of such centralisation to a previous epoch. If the term 'feudalism' is to have any meaning at the level of political structure then it must be associated with the parcellisation of sovereignty. To dub a centralised state as 'feudal' in the sense of continuous with previous state forms can lead only to a reworking of historical data to accommodate the dislocations that arise.

Despite then the higher level of sophistication that Dobb's *Studies* had brought to discussion of the economic nature of the transition from feudalism to capitalism, the discussions of 1947–48 resulted in a simple repetition of the crude generalisations about classes and political change that had been expressed in 1940–41. In some cases the sharper identification of class forces that Dobb had made possible was either ignored or simply reworked into the basic political model; on the other hand, the deviations that Dobb had committed from the work of Marx on the periodisation of capitalist development went largely unnoticed.

Later articles in the *Communist Review*, for example those of Joseph and Clark in 1949, simply re-iterated the lines of argument on the politics of the seventeenth century already expressed in 1940–1, and no development in this direction in fact occurred. Within the rubric of Marxist history however no development could take place, since any refinement of the periodisation laid down by Marx and Engels had necessarily to violate the relation they had established between economics and politics. Only the 'dialectic' intervened to provide protection against a direct reduction of political relations to economic relations, and as we have seen the dialectic operated more as a time-lag than anything else. It was possible for Dobb to 'refine' the periodisation established in *Capital* because, within limits, this could be presented as modification on the basis of more modern research. Attempts to examine the political sphere however were circumscribed by a doctine which argued that the principle forces at work there had their foundations in the economy. To move away from this constant 'referring back' in the investigation of political forces was to run the risk of being branded a reformist and non-Marxist. In the political climate of the late forties and early fifties this presented Marxist intellectuals working on history with a dilemma; and in the Communist Party the increasing pressure against any kind of theoretical or intellectual activity added to these problems. Before *Communist Review* was closed the writing skills of historians like Rodney Hilton were employed in composing pieces on 'peaceful co-existence', while the *Modern Quarterly* was shut down in 1953 by Palme Dutt's announcement to a startled editorial board that there was no place for intellectual work in the Party.

It is not surprising then that those British historians who survived this period as 'Marxists' worked on areas which did not involve a serious consideration of political history. And it is quite understandable that Hilton should wish to forget the history of the Transition debate as one beginning in 1940, and in presenting the material from *Science and Society* and elsewhere characterise the problems chiefly in terms of economic history.

Ironically the points that were made be Sweezy respecting the nature of the economics of the transition period revived the controversy over the nature of the pre-revolutionary state; but, partly because some of his critics were foreign, the theoretical stakes involved were suppressed in favour of an academic debate. In effect this third round of the Transition debate resolved itself into arguments over the theory and history of capitalist development conceived as an *economic* evolution, and thus strengthened the apparent relation to *Studies in the Development of Capitalism*. Since the arguments presented have almost without exception been encountered before, this phase of the debate can be dealt with fairly rapidly.

Sweezy criticised *Studies'* equation of feudalism with serfdom, which was defective because it did not treat feudalism as a specific *system* of production which might or might not be associated with serfdom. Instead of this, he put forward the conception of feudalism as characterised by production for use, rather than exchange. Intra-village exchange takes place, but long-distance trade plays no role in the process of production.

This version of feudal production is supported by a quotation from *Capital* Volume 1 (Sweezy 1976a, p. 35). It is argued that to oppose production for use to production for exchange as fundamental features of economic systems is not to suggest for example that trade and exchange do not exist in the former, merely that their role is strictly circumscribed. Thus, Sweezy asserts, he is not treating feudalism as a natural economy.

Dobb had argued that the collapse of feudal production was the result of internal contradictions; Sweezy on the other hand suggests that the tendencies identified by Dobb which produced such a breakdown were in fact historical developments engendered externally to the feudal system itself (Sweezy, 1976a, p. 41). The 'external explanation' for the collapse is resolved in effect to the consequences of long-distance trade, which placed production for use and production for exchange in a state of economic competition which the former could not win.

Following on from this, it is only logical that Sweezy should identify trade as the means of dealing with the gap existing between the decline of feudalism and the rise of capitalism (rejecting the suggestion that a feudal order survived to the seventeenth century, which is at times suggested in *Studies*). Anyone familiar with the debates of the 1940s knows how to deal with this of course, and Dobb in his reply succintly stated the by-now well-worn response:

> The crucial question which Sweezy has apparently failed to ask (or if he has, he would seem to have burked the answer to it) is this: what was the ruling class of the period? Since (as Sweezy himself recognises) there was not yet developed capitalist production, it cannot have been a capitalist class. If one answers that it was something intermediate between feudal and capitalist, in the shape of a bourgeoisie which had not yet invested its capital in the developmnet of a bourgeois mode of production, then one is in the Pokrovsky-bog of 'merchant capitalism'. If a merchant bourgeoisie formed the ruling class, then the state must have been some kind of bourgeois state. And if the state was a bourgeois state already, not only in the sixteenth century but even at the beginning of the fifteenth, what constituted the essential issue of the seventeenth century civil war? It cannot (according to this view) have been *the* bourgeois revolution. (Dobb, 1976, p. 62)

When Sweezy tried to argue that perhaps the sixteenth-century was pluralist, the point was repeated by Hill, citing the support of Soviet and English historians in his assertion that the absolute monarchy was a form of feudal state (1976, p. 120). This position was still repeated by Dobb in a lecture on the transition debate during the 60s (1967, p. 15).

The continual re-emergence of doubts as to the nature of the pre-revolutionary state was linked to the production of a 'gap' in the chronology of feudalism and capitalism that Dobb had pointed to in 1946. This hole in the evolution of economic formations was dealt with in two ways: either by asserting that feudal forms dominated until 1640 despite the emergence of capitalist forms, albeit in non-strategic sectors; or by seeking in the politics of the sixteenth century a more suitable state form. To do the latter was however to suggest that non-productive forms of capital (merchant capital) could be represented in a state and form an alliance with feudal interests, creating in a sense a progressive feudal state. This had the effect of liquidating the political historiography of the English revolution, and was therefore always rejected in favour of the first solution, despite some obvious problems. It is significant that no historian sought to elaborate the nature of this seventeenth-century feudal monarchy in the course of the debate – instead, historical evidence was directed to the character of the feudal economy, in contributions from Hilton, Takahashi and Hibbert (1976 and 1953).

But it is the manner in which political forms were simply deduced form the interests of economic classes that itself produced this gap in the chronology of transition. Treating the evolution as *economic* in principle, facilitated or hindered by the mode of representation of class forces at the level of a (centralised) state, the pace of the transition was of course hard to account for as long as political forces retained this merely expressive role. The reflex of Marxist historians in such a situation is to develop the analysis of economic history in order to solve a problem which in fact requires some thought on political institutions and their foundations.

This can be illustrated by the later work of Hobsbawm and Hilton. The former for instance published in 1954 a long article in two parts which sought to explain why, given that capitalist forces were unleashed in seventeenth-century Europe, the industrial revolution did not occur until the later eighteenth century (1954a, p. 39). This 'final phase in the transition from feudalism to capitalism' was blocked by a General Crisis of the European economy, argues Hobsbawm. Lublinskaya, in her critique of this thesis, had demonstrated that the evidence for such a general crisis is dubious and that other economic factors can be advanced to explain the 'delay' (1968, p. 64). But here again, the question of the development of capitalist relations and their chronology is dealt with as though an autonomous history exists for them within a given social formation, and the transformations that they undergo are the result of, and explicable by, purely economic forces. While lip-service is paid to the role of political and other forces in this evolution, it has been shown that in the Transition debate the function of such (external or derivative) forces was circumscribed by what is in effect a crude base-superstructure model of social formations. As will be suggested below, all such models are in the last instance similar, and attempts to develop some sophistication generally result in a departure from the explanatory rigour of Marxist analysis.

Hilton's more recent *Bond Men Made Free* is another example that serves to show the order of explanation adopted by English Marxist historians when dealing with political forces. For this account of the rising of 1381 begins with a lengthy account of the medieval rural economy whose function is to identify the formation of different classes and indicate the terrain on which their struggles are projected. The identification of the nature of political conflict depends on a prior understanding of the conflicts existing in the economy, while both polity and economy are constituted in a manner which assumes their logical separation and the subordination of the former to the latter.

Hobsbawm and Hilton are of course representative of a more orthodox Marxism than those modern writers who seek to deal with historical problems in terms of Marxist theory, or develop historical aspects of Marx's work. Two such recent contributions – from Brenner and Anderson – will now be briefly considered, with the object of showing that despite the diversity of these texts, there can be detected a common residual of problems similar in kind to those found in the Transition debate.

In 1976 *Past and Present* published an article by Brenner which sought to emphasise the class-based nature of agrarian evolution in early modern Europe. A series of replies from prominent historians were published during 1978, chiefly criticising the manner in which Brenner utilised historical evidence. The general theses advanced were not subjected to any lengthy scrutiny, and it was not generally noted that much of what Brenner was arguing had already been suggested in *Studies in the Development of Capitalism.* In some respects indeed the article read in parts as an exercise in updating the earlier text, and many of the adversary positions are in fact common to Dobb and Brenner. Postan for instance suggested that Brenner's criticisms of 'demographic' explanations of the medieval economy were repetitions of those made by Kosminsky and Barg (Postan 1978, p. 25), and it is true that some of the arguments put forward by Brenner concerning rents and prices can be found in an earlier article by Kosminsky (1955, pp. 16–19). Another problem that Brenner encountered was his reliance on sometimes-outdated sources for his analysis of Eastern Germany, a point on which Heide Wunder corrected him (1978). Only one substantial supporter of Brenner contributed to the symposium and he criticised Brenner for a 'political Marxism' which impoverished his formulation of the feudal mode of production (Bois, 1978, p. 67).

Brenner identified two main 'deviations' in accounts of the medieval economy, the 'demographic model' and the 'commercialisation model'. As we have seen, neither of these are 'foreign to Marxism', in that Dobb used demographic explanations of economic change in places, and Sweezy had recourse to trade effects in the explanation of the decline of feudalism. It is however the former, represented in the writings of Postan and Le Roy Ladurie, that is the principle problem for Brenner, since he argues that these writers have in fact themselves powerfully attacked commercialisation models. The problem however is that both writers, having demolished market-centred explanations of economic change, proceeded to put demography where previously was trade in historical arguments. Further, Postan did not identify what is for Brenner the 'fatal flaw' of trade-centred arguments, the neglect of feudalism as a *relation of power* in which it is the arbitrariness of the exactions that is the important factor, not simply their economic form.

This follows from the earlier declaration that

> it is the structure of class relations, of class power, which will determine the manner and degree to which particular demographic and commercial changes will affect long-run trends in the distribution of income and economic growth – and not *vice versa*. (Brenner, 1976, p. 31)

Brenner then proceeds to outline what is in effect a 'horizontal' and a 'vertical' theory of class relations: the former between direct producers, their tools and the land in the direct process of production; and the latter between relations of property, underwritten by force, ensuring the extraction of surplus. Broadly speaking, developments in economic formations are the result of changes in these relations, and rents, prices, population growth and wages merely reflect this.

In the latter part of the article, the demands of this perspective are measured against two problems of comparative history: why there was a differential evolution in property forms in West and East Germany; and why in Britain a system of capitalist agriculture based on tenant farming arose as a dominant form while in France agricultural production was dominated by sharecropping and dwarf peasant holdings? On both these counts later contributors made serious criticisms of the evidence advanced, but here it is only necessary to note that the problem posed by Brenner addressed itself to the question of transition conceived as a process of economic evolution. In effect, since transformative power in his model is ascribed only to 'class struggle' arising on the basis of given economic relations, there is the tendency to deal with all change as reducible to economic forces alone. In a very real way then Brenner follows on from the kind of approach adopted in *Studies in the Development of Capitalism*, in that what he is concerned to do is elucidate the economic genealogy of capitalism. Although the theoretical approach is in 1976 relatively crude, it is the 'history' that is the major concern. But this history always runs the risk of being written off by specialists, and while in *Studies* the theoretical depth of the text meant that it was always more than a target for historical criticism, this is not the case with Brenner. A similar problem in the work of Wallerstein has been located by Theda Skocpol, who has pointed out that once the plethora of data deployed in *The Modern World System* is stripped away, all that is left is a simple teleological account of capitalist development in which political forces are functional expressions of class interests (Skocpol, 1977).

Attention was drawn at the beginning of this essay to Perry Anderson's commitment to genealogy in the analysis of the capitalist structure of Britain, and the continuation of this project in *Passage from Antiquity to Feudalism* and *Lineages of the Absolutist State* has been forcefully stated in Hirst's review (1975). While it is unnecessary then to devote much space to this aspect of Anderson's project, some comments can be made concerning the manner in which mode of production and state are conceived – for Anderson seeks to break away from orthodox Marxist accounts of economy and politics and develop alternative explanations of absolutism to those met already.

At one level it appears that the break that is made is quite radical. Rejecting the conventional account of modes of production as constitutive of the economic level of social formations, he instead inserts 'superstructural elements' into the heart of his definition of pre-capitalist modes of production, while maintaining that the analysis is to be developed in terms of politics rather than economics. Pre-capitalist states are differentiated not by forms of economic base, but rather according to variant organisation of political and legal superstructures. This is justified by the statement that 'it is the constructon and destruction of States which seal the basic shifts in the relations of production, so long as classes subsist' (Anderson, 1974b, p. 11). Accordingly, the analysis of pre-capitalist state and politics must needs focus on legal and political forces, and not the structure of economies, organised by Marxist concepts of modes of production.

The manner in which Anderson deals with the Marxist theoretical principles that underlay previous analyses of bourgeois revolutions and the absolutist state is in fact severely defective, and on this count alone it would be possible to show that where Anderson purports to elaborate basic theoretical propositions he in fact misconceives them and proceeds to reduce them to the level of ideal-typical constructs in a comparative sociology. It can quite easily be shown then that Anderson has more in common with Weber and Hintze than Marx (Skocpol and Fulbrook, 1977, p. 295). But paradoxically Anderson is at the same time committed to the basic relation of economics and politics that is banished by his reluctance to examine the determining role of the economy. For determine it does, in a most classic way, even theough it is offstage during the course of a magisterial progression through the courts of early modern Europe. Far from breaking away from orthodox Marxist accounts of transition, then, Anderson simply repeats some of its most classic conceptions. For where do his states come from? They turn out, in the Western case, to be representations of class forces, and these class forces are in fact categories drawn from an economic level which is nowhere examined in the two volumes. In the chapter 'The Absolutist State in the West' which prefaces *Lineages'* international tour, a series of categories such as the bourgeoisie, the nobility, the peasantry and merchant capitalists are related to the form in which the absolutist state arises. While vague, such categories are deployed as economic classes either represented in or excluded from the structure of the state, and the domain of the political is thus constituted in the familiar guise of the region in which classes defined according to economic categories conflict. The state organises this domain as one controlled by dominant classes, although as we have seen above there is usually space allowed for discrepancies between the interests of dominant economic classes and the structure of the state. In a genealogical history however this discrepancy is simply utilised to explain the rate at which the structure evolves towards the present, making possible the clarification of 'delays' and 'accelerations' in the trajectories that Anderson presents.

This essay has sought to identify two major problems in the writing of Marxist history in Britain. The first is a commitment to the analysis of contemporary capitalism through the method of a genealogy; the second is the attempt to treat political forces as simply derivative, secondary to prior economic forces. We have seen that this latter problem has two major variations: the exclusion of direct discussion of political forms and the concentration on the structure of economic relations (an enterprise in which the names of Dobb and Hindess and Hirst become linked, for in *Pre-Capitalist Modes of Production* politics lives only in the interstices of 'class struggle' and the 'conjuncture'); or a concentration on politics, but in which the political sphere is merely an expression of pre-given economic relations.

In part at least the genealogical method has followed from the impact of Marx's own discussions of English capitalist development, and the cost of fighting free of this for Marxist history has perhaps been the liquidation of a commitment to Marxism. The problem of the origin of capitalism, however, conceived in terms of a transition from feudalism, still flourishes in the ranks of contemporary historians, albeit not as a fundamental issue confronting historical writing.

This quest for the origins of capitalism is generated by the conception of capitalism as a totality, whose (historically given) structure is only knowable through analysis of its genesis. The sought-after genealogy of capitalism as a means for the interpretation of the present is the genealogy of a totality; for Marxists, committed to the determining role of the economy in the analysis of social formations, the essence of this historically given totality is to be located in the unrolling of the economic relations of capitalist society.

The question of the transition from feudalism to capitalism

consequently assumes a central importance, since this process of transition is at the same time the moment of the genesis of a totality, capitalism. We have seen above however that once a rigorous Marxist account of the economic relations of this process is initiated, serious lapses appear in the fabric of this genealogy – the process of transition at the economic level is revealed as one that unrolls spasmodically and not always in the prescribed direction. The reasons for this unevenness are not apparent in the economy, and Dobb dealt with this problem by leaving a yawning gap of 200 years between the dominance of the economic relations of feudalism and the dominance of the economic relations of capitalism.

The gap was however tentatively closed, through the invocation of politics. The Marxist precept, 'the class struggle is the motor of history' is inserted between the shafts of the feudal wagon and is encouraged to drag the immobile economic order of feudalism into capitalism through periodic dialectical interventions. But this 'politics' on closer inspection turns out to be constituted by a projection of economic relations onto a space which they already occupy: politics is used to explain the contradictory progress of the economic order, but it is itself no more than an expression of this order. Notwithstanding such difficulties, 'politics' does the job, the gap between feudalism and capitalism is closed and an orderly genesis is re-established.

But it has also been noted that the political form which performs this task is the 'feudal-absolutist state', suited for the role on account of its character as a centralising and mediating apparatus. 'Absolutism', as a historian's category, is identified as a suitable candidate for effecting the difficult birth of capitalism because it has as its major characteristic the *centralisation* of political forces. And so, just as socialism follows capitalism as an economic order because socialism is a rational form of the centralisation of capitalist monopoly, so absolutism is endowed by the questing historian with the necessary powers of transforming economic relations which at times seem to be reluctant to properly evolve into capitalist forms. The problem of the totality-to-be is solved by introducing centralised political forces which are capable of cohering diverse social and economic forces in a new historical totality, capitalism.

While the Transition debate dealt apparently with a historical problem, it has been suggested above that the central issue that generated its problems for discussion involved the failure of Marxists to confront political forces as anything other than an expression of economic relations. As has also been suggested, this problem has its source in that this was the method prescribed by Marx in his writings. It is notable that English Marxists have been content to repeat formulations to the effect that the Tudor state was 'feudal-absolutist' without any serious study being undertaken of the nature of the absolutist monarchies of Europe in terms of the reorganisation of political domain that they involve. Lublinskaya's work on France, and Brunner's on Austria, demonstrate that serious questions arise in these orders which are not reducible to a simple representation of class forces. The absolutist state should not be treated in this way not least because it embodies a conception of sovereignty which haunts modern 'Marxist' theories of the state, in which the state is rendered in the image of the absolute monarch. It is indeed ironic that Anderson's project should be aimed at demonstrating the absolutist nature of the pre-revolutionary Tsarist regime, when the conception of state and politics in modern democracies is organised by modern socialists along the lines of an absolute monarchy.

The great achievement of Marx was to develop, out of legalistic foundations, an *economic* conception of social organisation.[3] Civil society was transformed, as Brunner has suggested (1977, p. 165), into an economic social formation, in which however many of the economic categories were implicated in legal categories – such as possession, separation, commodity and property. The logico-historical method that dominates the narrative of *Capital* owes much to Savigny, as does the Romanic nature of Marx's concept of commodity. The problem however is that this novel juridico-economic constitution of social forms required that the constitution of political agents took place on the basic of this given juridico-economic domain. Membership of 'political society' was conditional upon an evaluation of the economic credentials possessed by agents, and the construction of institutions was licensed only by their expression of specifiable class interests. It might have been noted that the category 'bourgeoisie' was one of the means by which historians sought to escape the limitations of this model, since such a term belongs to a political discourse and unites a number of possible class representatives. The bourgeoisie however, whatever their composition, are invariantly related to capitalist forces, and consequently the economic identification of classes is only sidestepped at the cost of clarity. Marxist historians in England have sought to explain the origins of capitalism in order to develop the work of Marx, but within the analytical framework of Marx such a project is fraught with contradictions that render the outcome ambivalent.

2 The Structure of Agrarian Capitalism – The 'English Model'

2.1 INTRODUCTION

> In the history of primitive accumulation, all revolutions are epoch-making that act as levers for the capitalist class in course of formation; but, above all, those moments when great masses of men are suddenly and forcibly torn from their means of subsistence, and hurled as free and 'unattached' proletarians on the labour-market. The expropriation of the agricultural producer, of the peasant, from the soil, is the basis of the whole process. The history of this expropriation, in different countries, assumes different aspects, and runs through its various phases in different orders of succession, and at different periods. In England alone, which we take as our example, has it the classic form. (*Capital*, Vol. 1, pp. 669–70)

Marx never made the mistake of treating 'capitalism' as if it were a creature of the nineteenth century, personified by cities, factories, railways and the proletariat which inhabited this new realm. While he suggested that 'capitalist agriculture' could only develop effectively on the basis of machinery, fertilisers and other products supplied to agriculture by advanced industrial concerns, he argued that the historical basis for industry was itself to be found in the development of capitalist relations in agriculture, assuming its classic form in England. The chronology that he gave to this process began in the sixteenth century with enclosures, which initiated the separation of producers from the land that was the pre-condition for the establishment of a wage-earning proletariat, the form of labour appropriate to capitalism.

The consolidation of landholding and a transformation of independent 'yeoman' farmers into tenants of improving landlords completed the structure in which landlord, tenant and labourer were in the eighteenth century to find their place. As this structure became established it formed a home market for the products of manufacture, whose site of production shifted gradually to urban areas; thus in England the advance of the relations of capitalist agriculture was accompanied by a ruralisaton of the countryside and the creation of a new relationship between town and country. In the nineteenth century domination soon passed to the towns and cities which produced industrial commodities and accounted for the majority of the national population, eclipsing the previous hegemony of agriculture and the countryside.

Of course, there is no shortage of critics for Marx's scenario of English capitalist development, and objections have been levelled at the factors he emphasised (like enclosure and the proletarianisation of rural labour), and at the chronology into which they are inserted. At first glance virtually the whole of modern research into English agricultural history seems to place in question Marx's account of 'primitive accumulation'. But it is not as though modern historians reject the idea that the late seventeenth and early eighteenth centuries witnessed profound changes in agriculture; in fact substantial agreement exists on the existence of an agricultural revolution during this period, conceived however as increases in output consequent upon changes in organisation and techniques. Many writers seem anxious to demonstrate that such a transformation had little to do with a *capitalist* development of the rural economy, and in fact evidence is marshalled to disprove such an idea. Thus for example Marx is credited with the idea that capitalist enterprise requires large units of production; and since small units survive, or even perhaps flourish at the end of the eighteenth century, then this both shows that Marx was wrong and that English agriculture was non-capitalist in the eighteenth century.

This essay will show that this, and other arguments, rest both on an extremely rudimentary grasp of what capitalism in agricultural production looks like, and also an unfortunate tendency to cook the historical evidence so that arguments about the non-existence of rural wage-labour or the hardiness of small farmers can be sustained. Marx was correct when he identified the develment of capitalist relations in English agriculture as the 'classic model' of capitalist development, producing in the eighteenth century the dominance of agrarian capitalism in the economy as a whole. But while Marx was correct in his general lines of argument, there are elements in his genealogy of capitalism that are both historically wrong and theoretically dubious – for example the identification of rural surplus-labour as the source of the industrial proletariat. An outline of the capitalist nature of agriculture in eighteenth-century England that seeks to 'defend Marx' in the way that, for example, Lazonick (1974) does involves two limitations: arguments are tied to a justification of Marx's statements, with their associated strengths and weaknesses; and the organisation of material is dominated not by an exposition of the structure of capitalist relations, but by the structure of Marx's narrative. Lazonick 'applies Marx' with the objective of vindicating Marx, not with the objective of outlining the capitalist nature of the English agrarian economy. Moreover, as is noted above, a simple-minded confrontation of the 'facts' supplied by modern research with the propositions to be found in *Capital* Volume 1 can lead to the conclusion that Marx's account of capitalist agriculture is utterly erroneous. An instance of such an approach can be found in an article by Kins Collins, in which Marx's comments are converted into 'falsifiable hypotheses' *à la* Popper and the statements of agrarian historians wheeled in to deliver refutation after refutation (K. Collins, 1967). The theoretical rigour of this exercise does not of course extend to considering the agrarian historians as potential candidates for refutation, since they after all deal only with the realm of facts, and Collins knows full well that no problems exist there.

'Applying Marx's theory of capitalism' to the English countryside is not therefore a very satisfactory way of developing an account of agrarian capitalism. But since this means that resort to Marx for the occasional quotation (a convenient means of evading difficulty that is a reflex for every orthodox Marxist) is ruled out, the absence of the Master's voice leaves the definition of 'capitalism' somewhat obscure. It is to be hoped that in the following pages a relatively consistent usage will be adhered to, but it is appropriate here to make some remarks on the general characteristics of capitalism as a form of economic organisation dominant in the eighteenth-century English rural economy.

Capitalism can be briefly summarised as a form of economy in which consumption is separated from production, enterprises are separated and in a state of competition, and the national economy is co-ordinated according to the profitability of the commodities sold by enterprises. In the context under consideration here, this means that the capitalist farm, leased from a landlord by a farmer who supervises the labourers who work it, is an enterprise whose continued existence depends on the profitability of the commodities that it sells. Its consumers are the purchasers of its products, and while it produces certain crops for its own consumption (such as fodder), these are consumed not be those who work the farm, but by the process of production itself. Since the profitability of the commodities produced dominates calculation, the organisation of the farm and the composition of its output are determined by considerations of cost, time, ease of transport, and price of sale – sometimes put down to 'market forces', but that is a very inexact term. These differentiated conditons can be met by a diversity of enterprise forms, and so there is no general division between 'capitalist' and 'non-capitalist' enterprises, nor is the capitalistic character of an economy derivative of capitalist enterprises as its founding and essential elements. In principle then, the 'capitalist farm' could be either a large farm in which a farmer supervises wage-labourers, or a family farm in which family labour is supervised by a household head: the absence of wage-labour does not mean that a farm is non-capitalist. The criterion in such cases concerns the conditions of existence of the enterprise – if for example the farm employs no wage-labour, but concentrates on the production of fruit or dairy produce, it is inevitable that conditions of sale and the changing requirements of the household would only be stable so long as costs and prices were predictable. The construction of railways, or the development of large urban dairies, would bring a change in such conditions for the small dairy farmer, but the consequent calculations would in such cases be little different in character from those which had previously created a farm based on the sale of dairy produce as a commodity. In general then, capitalist economy involves 'production of commodities by means of commodities' and the dominance of forms of calculation to effect this; to identify 'capitalism' with a set of essential factors (wage-labour, large-scale production, 'the market') leads to serious problems when dealing with agrarian capitalist relations; and alternatively, to suppose that the capitalistic character of the enterprise can simply be deduced from prevailing 'capitalist forces' simply obscures the actual functioning of economic systems under rhetorical and general categories.

What then of the 'Agricultural Revolution'? The current orthodoxy identifies the principal revolutionary period as the latter half of the eighteenth century and the early part of the nineteenth, the Napoleonic Wars marking the transition from one phase to another. Indices such as the expansion of the national population and the increased output of wheat are linked to changes in field-courses, altered uses of manure, introduction of fodder-crops like turnips and clover, improvements in the plough, and so on. Dissent from this timetable and list of factors is expressed only by Kerridge, who in his *Agricultural Revolution* (1967) argues that the major developments comprising this revolution are in fact completed to all intents and purposes by the end of the seventeenth century (p. 15). In particular, he disputes the importance given to Norfolk farming in the characterisation of progressive farming, assuming that to do so is to suggest that Norfolk was simply the model for all subsequent improvements (p. 33). Instead, Kerridge identifies a different set of factors to those proposed by other historians, such as the floating of water meadows, the substitution of convertible husbandry for permanent tillage or permanent grass and shifting husbandry, the introduction of new fallow crops, marsh drainage, manuring and stock-breeding (p. 40). The chronology is summarised as follows:

> We make no bones about asserting that the agricultural revolution dominated the period between 1560 and 1767 and that all its main achievements fell before 1720, most of them before 1673, and many of them much earlier still. (p.328)

The problem with the precociousness of this timetable is that if such an early start was made, why did output and other factors remain relatively stable until well into the eighteenth century? There is no question that considerable advances were made in agricultural technique during the seventeenth century, but Kerridge assumes that 'revolutionary effects' flow automatically from the changes that he identifies. Furthermore, the later seventeenth and early eighteenth centuries are characterised by a significant lull in the publication of farming literature, generally indicative of the degree of activity in the rural economy, as Slicher van Bath has pointed out (1963, p. 219).

Kerridge has himself argued in a polemical article that such tracts were for the most part instructional texts for novices in the established arts of agriculture (1969, p. 465), and it might be expected that a period of rapid agricultural advance would see the publication of a number of such treatises, disseminated through newly founded agricultural societies. This phenomenon is true of the later eighteenth century; while at the beginning of the century those works that appeared were either focused on horticulture, fruit-growing and cider-making, or were simply reprints of earlier manuals (Tribe, 1978, pp. 64–5).

Mingay, in a reply to Kerridge, pointed out that the latter's list of privileged factors in agricultural change omitted some important features of nineteenth-century agriculture, or rather discounted them altogether – for example, ignoring underdrainage, guano and artificial fertilisers, oil-cake feeding and the supplementing of turnips with other root crops (Mingay, 1969. p. 479). Seeking to preserve a privileged set of factors which are held to be constitutive of an agricultural revolution, rather than the pre-condition for it, Kerridge is led to discount the significance of some of the elements which marked the major phase of advance of capitalist agriculture in Britain. As F. M. L. Thompson has argued, the period 1750–1815, with which we are principally concerned here, is one typified mainly by the combination of new forms of management with the rise of the self-sufficient farm as the unit of production (Thompson, 1968, pp. 63–5). The 'technical factors' which the majority of agricultural historians place in the centre of attention are in fact subsidiary to the significance of management and farm in the later eighteenth century.

In the account that follows, attention will be focused mainly on arable crops, rather than meat, poultry, wool, hops or fruit. This is in part merely a reflection of a bias in the literature on agricultural history, but can be justified to some extent by the significance of wheaten bread as the staple of the bulk of the national population. It is perhaps more important to note that an emphasis on arable cultivation encourages the conception of agricultural produce as food or fodder, whereas it also includes 'industrial' crops which are either subject to processing before consumption (like hops), or which are not edible at all (like wool and hides). The purpose of this essay is, however, not to write a history of capitalist agriculture, rather it aims to elucidate the capitalist features of the eighteenth-century economy, and for such a purpose arable production is sufficient.

2.2 ESTATE, FAMILY AND TENANCY IN THE EIGHTEENTH CENTURY

Until about twenty years ago, it was usual to attribute the agricultural advances of the eighteenth century to the dynamism of improving landlords such as Coke of Holkham and Townshend of Raynham; whether driven by rapacity or ideals, the result was the same. This picture of eighteenth-century agriculture dominated by the activities of progressive landlords can be found in Ernle's *English Farming, Past and Present*, a work first published in 1912 and which also placed its faith in the reliability of Board of Agriculture reports and husbandry tracts as historical sources. Since the 1950s, however, a number of historians have, on the basis of unpublished data and county archives, shown that the account provided by Ernle is seriously defective, and have proposed an alternative model of the agriculture of the period, directing attention to the technicalities of farming practice and away from the social structure of the countryside.

The history of agriculture that results from this is consequently as impoverished in its own way as the discredited history of Ernle. For rentier landlordism left its mark indelibly on the rural economy of the eighteenth century, and its relegation to a peripheral role in the analysis of agrarian relations only promotes a technicism inherent in modern histories. The accumulation of farmland under the control of a relatively small group had the effect of centralising flows of resources in agricultural production, and, in the absence of financial institutions able to offer credit to independent farmers, made possible the direction of investment into the agricultural sector. The process of estate consolidation that characterised the eighteenth century in certain regions, itself the result of familial and political imperatives, made available to prospective tenants consolidated farms together with a docile labour force which was in many ways tied to the estate. It would be misleading, therefore, to consider landlords only as consumers living off the backs of capitalist farmers and wage-labourers, as if they were in some sense redundant in the scheme of things and able to subsist only by the ruthless exploitation of their landed property. This does not mean of course that one need agree with Curtler's view of them expressed in a criticism of the Hammonds, according to which the gentry were 'essentially lovers of country life, engaged in the management of their estates, fond of their open-air sports, good friends with their tenants, leading in fact a happy, wholesome, useful life' (Curtler, 1912, p. 292). An emphasis on the significance of the role of landlordism in the eighteenth-century agrarian economy does not imply a justification of their extravagance and waste, rather it seeks to understand the effects that this had.

It is usual to include in the category 'landed class' both peers and gentry, although this does not exhaust the number of landholders, which included in addition small owners and institutions. The importance of the landed class was however marked by its association with family estates, areas of landholding which provided revenue, residence and identity through the generations (Habakkuk, 1953, p. 2). Mingay suggests that an income of £10,000 per annum was required to maintain the social position of the four hundred top landowners, which if flowing entirely from rentals, would indicate that each held an estate of 10–20,000 acres. In fact the majority of landlords in this class did rely on their agricultural rents, rather than on offices, mineral exploitation or urban rents, and thus the assumption can be made that they as a whole controlled over 20 per cent of the cultivated land in England and Wales (Mingay, 1963, pp. 19–20). The income of the next social group, the wealthy gentry, would have to have been £3–4000 per annum, this group comprising around seven or eight hundred families; while the lesser gentry, perhaps three or four thousand families, would have commanded an income of £1–3000 per annum. Taken together these three categories account for 75 per cent of the cultivated land at the end of the eighteenth century, a figure worth bearing in mind when discussion turns below to the question of small farmers in the agrarian economy. Landlords of one kind or another controlled the bulk of farming land in the eighteenth century, and their policies with respect to this land are crucial in an assessment of the structure of agriculture in this period.

The relative significance of agriculture in the national economy during this period can be judged from the figures presented in Table 2.1, which is itself based on the estimates of Gregory King and Arthur Young. An alternative estimate made in 1811 by Colquhoun suggested that agriculture accounted for 50 per cent of the national capital stock, which although possibly inaccurate, indicates a continuing dominance of agricultural production in the early nineteenth century (Pollard, 1968, pp. 338–9).

Perhaps most significant in these figures is the indication that, while 'manufacturing' grew rapidly between the later seventeenth and the later eighteenth centuries, it did no more than keep roughly in step with the growth in agriculture and commerce. Not until after the end of the Napoleonic Wars did the role of agriculture begin to decline in the national economy, whether measured in employed populations or output by value. To discuss the agrarian economy of the eighteenth century is to discuss the dominant sector in the national economy. And this agrarian economy was in turn dominated by a class of large landowners.

The eighteenth-century landed estate was the physical site of a family, and the importance of this family became expressed in the building and rebuilding of country houses, fashioning around them a landscape from which the house became the object of a

TABLE 2.1. The structure of the National Product in the eighteenth century (England and Wales)

	c. 1688		*c. 1770*	
	£m.	*% of N.I.*	*£m.*	*% of N.I.*
Agriculture	19.3	40	58.2	45
Manufacture, Mining, Building	9.9	21	30.3	24
Commerce	5.6	12	17.0	13
Professions, Domestic Service	7.4	15	14.9	11
Government and Defence	3.3	7	5.7	4
Rent of Housing	2.5	5	4.0	3
Total Product	48.0	100	130.1	100

(*Source*: Deane and Cole, 1962, p. 156, Table 35)

series of prospects. The cost of such work was considerable: Holkham Hall was built between 1732 and 1765 at a total cost of £92,000 for house, park, garden, lake and woods (Parker, 1975, p. 24). The long period over which the building took place made possible the financing of the project out of income, although the average yearly outlay of £2700 was not in fact expended year by year, but rather in fits and starts. F. M. L. Thompson has suggested that the impact of such large-scale building works materially contributed to the development of a variety of trades, employing large numbers of labourers and stimulating industrial enterprises at a crucial period in their growth (1969, pp. 57–8); while reservations might be made of such conclusions, it would be wrong to dismiss such projects as a diversion of resources into conspicuous consumption without considering the extensive effects such expenditure undoubtedly had on the economy as a whole.

The building of country houses was not the only major drain on the resources of landed families, for the purchase of land was also important for a number of reasons. First of all, social prestige dictated that the land in the immediate vicinity of the house should belong to the family: but this was also advantageous politically (arising from the control of potential voters) and economically (the consolidation of estate lands meant more efficient management and compact farms). These advantages did not however result in the tendency of families to concentrate all their holdings of land in one consolidated block, because the exigencies of marriage and inheritance demanded that separate estates by reserved for future use. Clay for example has shown how Sir Harbottle Grimston made every effort to buy out alien islands of land around his Hertfordshire estate at Gorhambury, while making no effort to concentrate the very scattered holdings of land in Suffolk and Essex (Clay, 1966, pp. 47–8, 56). With the development of a national marriage market this tendency became more marked, so that there were at once centrifugal and centripetal tendencies operating in the geography of eighteenth-century landholding, in which the dictates of rational farming encountered the demands of dowries and portions. In the case of the Leicester estate, the purchase of land contiguous to the Holkham estate was carried forward regardless of the current state of the family's finances, and sometimes heavy purchasing continued after the accumulation of substantial debts (Parker, 1975, p. 27).

The domination of the landlord over the surrounding countryside was expressed in the relation of the country house to the landscape. The process of building houses fit for nobles was accompanied by the construction of landscapes fit for the houses. Professional landscapers, such as Brown, Repton and Kent, designed an environment according to the doctrines of space and perspective to be found in the painting of Claude and Poussin. Marshall, the agriculturalist, described the relation of house and landscape as follows:

> Notwithstanding, however, the nature of the place ought not to be sacrificed to the mansion; – the house must ever be allowed to be a principal in the composition. It ought to be considered as the centre of the system; and the rays of art, like those of the sun, should grow fainter as they recede from the centre. The house itself being entirely a work of art, its immediate environs should be highly finished; but as the distance increases, the appearance of design should gradually diminish, until Nature and fortuitousness have full possession of the scene. (1796, Vol. 1 p. 274)

Barrell has emphasised the way in which the eighteenth-century landscape was an object of a gaze in which the land was something to be viewed from a distance and in one direction only (1972, p. 23). The parkland surrounding the house was at the same time an object of regard from the house, and also an area supplied with sites of prospects of the house, where guests could either walk or ride in a carriage, at each site being met with a regulated perspective of the house and its environs. Within the grounds of a park there might also be constructed a folly, in some cases with resident hermit; and such edifices were constructed likewise according to an aesthetic derived from landscape painting, that of 'ruin value'.

But the significance of such an adjustment of the natural to Nature went beyond expenditure of resources or aesthetic considerations, for the ability to mould the countryside in this fashion was itself expressive of the domination of landed property. The creation of 'prospects' to be viewed from the house led in many cases to the clearing away of houses and sometimes whole villages which literally spoilt the view. At Wimpole Hall in Cambridgeshire, for intance, Capability Brown supervised the demolition of a village between 1762 and 1772 (Taylor, 1973, pp.

164–5), and earlier at Stowe Bridgeman had done the same (Hyams, 1971, p. 14). Parkland was extended over farming land, and boundaries were marked by hahas, sunken fences which did not interrupt the eye in its journey to the horizon.

The process which brought this specific relation of domination into existence must however also be considered. As already suggested, the accumulation of lands was stimulated by a combination of politics and the family, in which the latter was conceived as composed of dead, living and unborn members, for which suitable mechanisms of inheritance had to be arranged. The transformation of land into economic property was associated directly with the transmission of the family's assets intact through the generations, and the related exigencies of marriage settlements (Habakkuk, 1950, pp. 27–8).

Two vital legal mechanisms emerged in the seventeenth century, the strict settlement and the mortgage. In the former, the intervention of trustees guaranteed the descent of real property to unborn heirs, limiting the function of an eldest son to that of a tenant for life. This secured incomes to relatives excluded from direct inheritance according to the custom of primogeniture, and prevented the heir selling parts of the estate off to meet current expenditure. One example of this limited and conditional form of inheritance can be found in the Bridgewater settlement of 1803 where the income from the Bridgewater canal was settled for life on the Marquis of Stafford, without however giving him any control over the management of the canal itself. It was specified that on the death of the Marquis the revenue was to pass, not to his eldest son, but to his second son. This had the consequence then that the Stafford estate benefited from this income during the lifetime of the Marquis, but on his death the estate descended to the eldest son, while the revenue which had been largely used to develop the estate ceased – promoting the concentrated use of the Bridgewater income for investment during the Marquis' lifetime, so that on his death the estate should not suffer from a lack of income on its own account (Richards, 1973, p. 41).

Marriages were devised with the object of accumulating or consolidating lands, brides requiring portions, and wives jointures[1], from fathers and husbands respectively. The financing of such transactions required that an estate mortgaged for a portion should be secure against dispossession, and the recognition of the debtor's equity of redemption in the courts effected this (McGregor, 1961, pp. 110–17). Mortgages also were of importance to landlords in providing access to secure credit, providing means of accumulation through purchase in an increasingly fluid market.

The accumulation of great estates through marriage was not a one-way street, as Clay has stressed (1968). The same devices which were directed towards the preservation of family property intact could under certain conditions result in its dissolution, despite the operation of strict settlement. An owner without a male heir but with several daughters would usually divide the property up between them, while the death of an owner without children or near relatives raised the possibility of distant relatives dividing up the estate. The existence of a land market was based to some extent on the regularity of such occurrences at a time when it was common for women to die in childbirth and children to die of one disease or another.

Within this structure of marriage and intermarriage, it has sometimes been suggested that heiresses of commercial fortunes provided a means for the commercial and landed classes to become linked, providing incidentally the income for the salvage of landed debt burdens. This entry of a commercial bourgeoisie into the landed aristocracy would then offer some possibility of a convergence between landowners and capitalist entrepreneurs, accounting for the dynamism of agricultural production in the eighteenth century. This argument is largely hypothetical however: one recent study of the spouses of male nobility concluded that all marriages to commoner heiresses declined absolutely from 54 (1700–1719) to 42 (1760–1779) to 20 (1780–1799), representing respectively 48.7 per cent, 20.9 per cent and 11.0 per cent of all peer marriages (D. Thomas, 1972, p. 107, Table 8). The 'business' component of these exchanges was always small, most out-marriages being contracted with partners who could be classed as coming from the already-gentlemanly category. Where what could be described as a new bourgeoisie did enter the class of substantial landowners, the means used was purchase outright, not marriage. The foremost figures of the first generation of industrial capitalists, such as Darby, Boulton, Peel, Arkwright, Fielden, Strutt and Whitbread bought estates, often at the end of the active careers, and it took in some cases three generations for the 'industrial' origin of these estates to be dissolved (F. M. L. Thompson, 1963, p. 21). The sum involved was often high, relative to other costs: Arkwright for example offered £220,000 for the Leominster estate in Herefordshire in 1809, a sum which was equivalent to 60 per cent of the current gross capital investment for the entire British cotton industry (Jones, 1967, p. 67).

A number of conditions then promoted the formation and maintenance of large and medium-sized estates which relied primarily on the existence of tenant farmers for their revenue. Thus by the end of the eighteenth century capitalist tenant farmers dominated English agriculture, not because the tenancy system represented the most efficient and progressive contemporary framework for the development of agriculture, but as a consequence of a social and political system which led to the concentration of blocks of land in the hands of a few landowners who both lived in the countryside and depended on farming rents for their income. This stimulated an interest on the part of the landlord in having 'good' tenants, that is, successful and profitable farmers with a suitable capital, which was generally around £500 in stock and equipment. The large tenant farms were themselves subject to consolidation through inheritance and marriage, and it was in this way that the majority of really large farms were in fact formed (Mingay, 1962, pp. 478–9). In times of recession, landlords sought to protect such tenants and in fact engaged in capital outlay in order to retain suitable tenants on their farms (Jones, 1968, p. 211).

Only on a few estates did the income from non-agricultural sources exceed the income from the rent toll. Timber for example, while often used on the estate, could be sold – and indeed in this period it was increasingly needed in the form of charcoal by the iron industry. The introduction of coke smelting, while diminishing the demand for timber, increased the demand for coal and iron ore, but there were very few estates who were in a position to exploit this rapidly developing market. Even those estates in industrial areas did not necessarily rely chiefly, or even in the main, on 'industrial' revenues, as Richards has pointed out for the Stafford estates (1973, p. 427). The prominence of agricultural income over all others was true also of those with considerable investments in stocks – Clay has shown that Earl Cowper, despite substantial holdings of stocks and securities, obtained from them an income only slightly more than that flowing from agricultural rents (1966, pp. 186–7). Despite the higher rates of return that were typical of non-landed investment, the benefits of landholding went beyond the simple calculation of rates of return. Curiously enough, however, cases arose like that of Samuel Whitbread II who succeeded to the estate built up by his father in 1796 while still retaining his brewing interest. Comparison of the income from both sources (admittedly in the high-rent years of 1803–9) shows that 27 per cent of his gross income came on average from brewery profits, and 73 per cent from his estates (Rapp, 1974, p. 383).

Some writers have suggested that this convergence of income on a landed interest was counter-balanced by the engagement of landlords directly in industrial or quasi-industrial investment, such as the building of canals and roads. This view is largely unsubstantiated however. River improvement, for example, essential for the effective transport and marketing of agricultural produce, was usually supported by mercantile, and not landed, interests. While the improved marketing of produce was necessary both for the expansion of agriculture and the consequent rise in rental income, landowners were usually hostile to proposals for river improvement on the grounds that their lands were damaged by subsequent flooding and changes in water-level (Ward, 1974, p. 14). On the other hand the prospect of expanded production and better transport threatened local producers who had hitherto enjoyed a semi-monopoly secured to them by poor communications and high transport costs. Be that as it may, landowners were typically little involved in those canals which formed the framework of the canal system, investing if at all in in short agricultural and mineral lines which touched their concerns directly (Ward, 1974, p. 157).

In many ways however the search for an 'industrial role' for the landlords of eighteenth-century England has it origins in an anxiety to demonstrate their engagement with what is assumed to be the dominant economic event of the eighteenth century, the beginning of the Industrial Revolution. If landlords can be shown to have contributed to this, then it is possible to view the parks and country houses with more favour – after all, then, they did contribute to economic progress, and need not be written off as economic parasites. The third essay in this book will show that this conception of the Industrial Revolution is a mirage, more a product of historical discourse than of the eighteenth century. In any case, the treatment of landlords as somehow extraneous to the 'development of capitalism' has been shown to be a misconception. The significance of landlordism in the national economy is not to be measured by the contributions that they made to capital investment, but is rather to be judged from the manner in which they affected the organisation of the rural economy. It will be shown below that the pressures that led landlords to organise the leasing of their land in such a manner that large tenant farms became a favoured category had great significance for the development of English agriculture; and so the 'contribution' of the landlords is to be judged not by the level of their investment, but by the set of relations that their activities stimulated.

2.3 ENCLOSURE: REORGANISATION OF LANDSCAPE AND LABOUR

The rapid decline of agricultural output, the increasing dereliction of the countryside, but above all the development of organised protest on the part of agricultural labourers over pay and conditions directed attention to the late-nineteenth-century countryside. The response was twofold: on the one hand Radicals campaigned for the establishment of smallholdings setted with rural or urban labourers; and on the other, writers sought to explain the absence in the English countryside of the social group that dominated so much of continental farming and rural politics – the peasantry. Radicals proposed that a return to smallholding, breaking up the dominance of medium and large tenant farms in agriculture, represented a solution to the social problems of the urban slums, as well as to the ossified class relations of the countryside, reviving collective forms of land ownership that had been destroyed by the rise of capitalist farming. Slater for instance suggested that

> ...British agriculture must be democratised. By this I mean that the principle of collective ownership of the soil must be established or re-established; that agricultural co-operation must be revived in new forms suitable to modern conditions; that the ancient right of independent access to the soil of every tiller of it must be restored; that a career of industrial

advance in agriculture must be made possible for the competent worker. (1907, p. vii)

Even Ernle, spokesman for the Tory party on agricultural policy, advocated a peasant reorganisation of agriculture, although on the different grounds that this would have a stabilising effect on national politics. He did however oppose the idea that the required transformation could be introduced through legislative means.

What then had become of the independent peasantry and its communal use of the land? Once posed in this fashion, it became necessary to locate a mechanism that could account for the separation of cultivators from the land and a transformation of their property into the consolidated units of the eighteenth-century farms. Marx had already suggested a mechanism that could effect this, and in its chronology provide a measure of the pace of development of capitalist farming: the enclosure settlements of the sixteenth, seventeenth and eighteenth centuries. As we shall see below, 'enclosure' has two aspects, a physical and geographical one which is related to the recasting of cultivated plots or the extension of cultivation over waste land; and property aspect, the change of rights in common fields or the appropriation of common land previously used for grazing or turf-cutting. These two separate features are sometimes run together, and indeed a reliance on the enclosure movement as a means of explaining the development of capitalist agriculture and the formation of an industrial labour force (in the style of Marx) relies in large measure for its plausibility on this occurring.

Nevertheless, any serious consideration of the transformation of a landscape in which independent cultivators predominated, to one where landlords, tenant-farmers and agricultural labourers took their place, necessarily involved an investigation of the extinction of common rights, and this could in large part be attributed to the effects of enclosure awards (Hasbach, 1908, pp. 98–9). The Hammonds in their famous study *The Village Labourer 1760–1832* suggested that in the later seventeenth century 'England was in the main a country of commons and common fields; at the time of the Reform Bill, England was in the main a country of individualist agriculture and of large enclosed farms' (Hammond, 1911, p. 26); that which was already enclosed in the seventeenth century, they claimed, was either old enclosure or lords' demesne land, the common field system typifying the life of the villages of England. Of course, one of the problems here is that this confuses 'common' with 'open' field systems; another is that while enclosure is identified as the mechanism undermining the communality and independence of this village life, the genesis of the agricultural labourer in the eighteenth century is a result of an overestimation of the rate of enclosure in the eighteenth century resulting from an uncritical use of Parliamentary Acts of Enclosure as a source (an error to be found in *Capital* Volume 1). That a similar error has been made more recently in the 'New Economic History' of enclosure is simply baffling, rather than significant – although the data employed is characterised in large part by its antiquity (McCloskey, 1972).

A. H. Johnson's account of the demise of the independent owner-cultivator did not place such emphasis on the role of enclosure, referring to it as a symptom rather than a cause of the consolidation of holdings (1963, p. 106). While he discusses in some detail the enclosure movement of the sixteenth century, identified by Tawney as the origin of the shift to commercial agriculture (Tawney, 1912, pp. 183–4), Johnson argues that direct eviction was not usually the objective of the landlords, rather an increase in control of copyholders. Directed mostly at open fields, not waste or common, this first phase of enclosure resulted, especially in the Midland counties, in a change of use of agricultural land from corn to sheep runs (Johnson, 1963, pp. 71–3.) There was however developing pressure on small occupiers following this, but it was not until the eighteenth century that extensive enclosure of commons and waste took place according to Johnson, in which typically the whole parish was involved in a rationalisation of holdings that in reducing or abolishing commons or waste jeopardised the continued existence of small holders of land. Furthermore, in the Parliamentary enclosures of the later eighteenth century the settlement was subject to the assent of a majority by acreage, not by head; it was not surprising then that it was the landowners, capitalist farmers and clergy who tended to benefit from the negotiated settlement.

Instead of using the chronology of enclosures to account for the decline of the small landowner, Johnson used Land Tax assessments for 500 parishes drawn from a variety of farming countries. From this he concluded that the period in which the most rapid consolidation of estates took place, associated with a shrinkage in the number of small owners, was 1700–1785, after which there was some degree of stabilisation. The period of greatest pressure is located at the end of the seventeenth century and during the first half of the eighteenth (Johnson, 1963, p. 147). Only in general does this chronology match that of the Hammonds or Marx: relying as they did on the spate of Parliamentary Acts in the later eighteenth century, it was easy to suggest that the main effect of such enclosures was to expel labourers from the land and drive them to the developing industrial towns – a neat association of the rise of surplus labour in the countryside consequent on rationalisation with the rise of a demand for semi-skilled and unskilled labour in the new factories. There are of course a number of problems concealed in this schemata, which will be examined in greater detail below; here it is only necessary to stress the manner in which Johnson, writing in 1909, dislocated the patter of enclosure awards from that of rural differentiation. An article published a year later took the conclusions of Johnson somewhat further on the basis of a detailed study of Land Tax assessments, enclosure awards and manorial surveys for Oxfordshire, for which it was shown that the period of decline of 'yeoman farming' (i.e. independent small farmers) preceded 1760, and that is was highly likely that enclosures during this period were a result, rather than a cause, of the disappearance of small farms (Gray, 1910, p. 326).

Mingay, in his introduction to Gonner's *Common Land and Inclosure* (which was originally published in 1912) has emphasised the problems inherent in the writings of those who, in seeking the origin of a rural proletariat, and the extinction of a presumed original state of community, fail to distinguish between different phases of the enclosure movement, and between common land and open fields (Gonner, 1966, p. li). For the significance of the enclosure movement does not lie in a simple relationship between the recasting of an agrarian landscape, transforming the open world of the scattered strips to the closed world of the hedged fields of a farm and the separation of cultivators from the soil. In the first place, the landscape of enclosure had been typical of large areas of England before the sixteenth century – the square fields typical of Kent and the south-east were labelled 'Romanic' by Gray in his study of field systems because of their resemblance to the patterns of cultivation followed before the introduction of the heavy 'non-Mediterranean' ploughs (Gray, 1915, p. 418). Secondly, the spate of enclosures in the later eighteenth century, in many cases merely ratifying and tidying up earlier piecemeal alterations, set the seal on the transformation of the English landscape into one dominated by the Farm sited on its holdings. Paradoxically, this *increased* the demand for rural labour as will be shown later, which is another problem for the chronology of labour supplied by the Hammonds; but perhaps more significantly, the separation of the farmhouse from the village set the seal on the geographical dispersion of the classes in the rural economy begun by the removal of the landlords to houses surrounded by vast lawns and parklands. Henceforth the English village was to be a place where labourers lived, separated from the farms on which they worked, and the farmers for whom they worked; instances of villages within whose bounds farmsteads can be found are today generally limited to the parishes, like those of southern Cambridgeshire, which retained an open landscape well into the nineteenth century. The 'typical English village' is rarely more than two hundred years old, not because of the impermanence of rural building *per se*, but because the enclosures of the seventeenth and eighteenth centuries changed the spatial disposition of rural social relations.

'Enclosure' then, while not a simple phenomenon, is important for an understanding of the structure of agrarian capitalism in England – though not for the 'labour supply' sort of argument to be found at the beginning of the century and more recently taken up by American econometric historians like McCloskey (1975), Linneman (1978) and Philpot (1975). Some consideration of the organisation of field-systems – the sites of agricultural production – will show what kind of changes follow from enclosing.

Gray defined a field system as 'the manner in which the inhabitants of a township subdivided and tilled their arable, meadow and pasture land' (Gray, 1915, p. 3). There is a loose relationship between the topographical arrangement of such systems and property forms, although by no means as close as is often assumed; confusion thus arises from the assumption that the 'open fields' which preceded enclosure were farmed in common, and that the 'Three Field System' in its classic form was the traditional medieval structure which only disappeared with the efforts of the improvers. Not only is the medieval village given a 'three field' system, it is assumed that the fields were the basis of rotations, the one-year-in-three bare fallow being followed for each field in turn. This assumption led Gray for instance to distinguish two-field from three-field villages along the lines that the former left one-half of the arable fallow each year, and the latter one-third, a distinction that only arises in this way if it is assumed that fields, rather than plots within each field, rotate (Baker, 1965, p. 88).

Since the land was farmed in strips, it was in fact these which formed the real basis of any rotation, and there was no overriding reason for the strips of any one field to follow a similar course of cultivation. The idea that the scattering of one individual's strips through the fields of a village was symptomatic of a communal allocation of dispersed plots arranged according to fertility and distance was explicitly rejected by one of the earliest studies of open-field organisation, the genesis of such a dispersal of a cultivator's land being traceable to accidents of inheritance, assarting,[2] or parcelling out of demesne (Orwin and Orwin, 1967). There is furthermore no reason to assume that each 'land' represented the property of one individual, since two or three lands could be placed together to form the 'strip' of one cultivator. Thus the units of landholding (the 'strip') should not be confused with the long, narrow lands created by heavy ploughs with mouldboards which formed the ridge-and-furrow landscape associated with the open fields. The contention of the Orwins, that such a system of farming was ubiquitous in medieval times, has been largely rejected by historians and geographers, who confine this form of farming to the Midlands (Baker and Butlin, 1973, pp. 621–2).

The terminology applied to different systems of farming is itself used in varying ways, with much resulting confusion, as we have seen with the use of 'common field'. Thirsk has sought to clarify the different features in the following manner, characterising a common field system as:

(1) Division of arable and meadow into strips among cultivators, each of whom may occupy a number of strips scattered about the fields.

(2) Both arable and meadow thrown open for common pas-

turing by the stock of all the commoners after harvest and in fallow seasons. This dictated that on the arable land some rules about cropping had to be observed, so that for example spring and winter-sown crops could be grown in different areas.

(3) Existence of common pasturage and waste, where the cultivators of strips have the right to graze stock, gather timber, cut peat, and have access to other materials, like stone and coal, as and where they are available.

(4) Ordering of the activities associated with this system by an assembly of cultivators – the manorial court, or where appropriate, a village meeting (Thirsk, 1964, p. 3).

While outlining these elements as those typical of a medieval common field system, Thirsk does not suggest that they all emerged together or that there was any necessary functional relation among them. Evidence for communal regulation is particularly thin, while the use of common and waste for grazing is perhaps the oldest. Furthermore, by making such distinctions in function, she is able to throw some light on the different field systems identified by Gray and explained by him according to diversity of origin. Thirsk suggests that in the case of villages either with one or more than three fields, the major activity of such examples was pasture, as opposed to arable farming, making redundant the discriminations outlined above where stock rearing was the principal concern (Thirsk, 1964, p. 23). It can be seen that much of the confusion in the discussion of the genesis of enclosure arises from the projection of a fully-fledged system (points (1)–(4)) that operated in some areas during the sixteenth century back into early medieval Britain as though it were a traditional and harmonious system of farming only destroyed by the onset of commercialisation.[3]

The fact that lands lying in open fields could be held in severalty led to some enclosure as a simple act of consolidation and marking of boundaries; but aside from this, 'enclosure' is used to refer to changes in use, or the fencing-in of arable, permanent meadow, commons and waste. The enclosure of waste was most destructive for the cottager, while the enclosure of meadow or arable naturally had different effects according to the structure of the village and the type of farming predominating. This has been succinctly summarised by Thirsk:

> To enclose land was to extinguish common rights over it, thus putting an end to all common grazing. To effect this, it was usual for the encloser to hedge or fence the land. Thus in contemporary controversy anger was directed mainly at the hedges and fences – the outward and visible signs of enclosure. To make it economically worthwhile, enclosure was often preceded by the amalgamation of several strips by exchange or purchase. If the enclosed land lay in the common arable fields or in the meadows, the encloser now had complete freedom to do what he pleased with his land throughout the year, instead of having to surrender the stubble or aftermath after harvest to the use of the whole township. On the pasture commons, enclosure by an individual signified the appropriation to one person of land which had previously been at the disposal of the whole community throughout the year. All enclosures, then, whether they concerned land in the common fields, in the meadows, or in the common pastures, deprived the community of common rights.
>
> (Thirsk, 1967, pp. 200–1)

While it might be associated with 'engrossing', the amalgamation of two or more farms into one (which in turn implies at least a degree of already-established enclosure), the two processes are in fact distinct. Further, it would be wrong to assume that enclosure in the sixteenth century was always conducted against the wishes of the interested parties, even though legislation was formulated to restrict changes in land use (Beresford, 1961).

Much of the enclosure carried out in the sixteenth century was for the purpose of creating sheep walks, but there was a decline in the demand for wool in the later part of the century; while then in many cases the conversion of arable to pasture land was the objective, the association of enclosure with depopulation, 'sheep eating men', was not universal either geographically or throughout the century. Much of the enclosure by agreement of the later sixteenth century, and throughout the seventeenth, was simply enclosure for the sake of better regulation of arable by individual cultivators. In this movement of course the smaller owners, as noted above, tended to lose the marginal rights that were essential for their survival, while no comparable major changes were felt by more substantial holders of land (Thirsk, 1959).

It would also be wrong to assume that the enclosures of the sixteenth century were significant as a major instrument of agricultural improvement. While the participants of the Midland rising of 1607 directed much of their wrath towards the hedges of the improvers, farming practice continued to be dominated by 'careful husbandry', in which advances derived from the better application of already well-tried methods. In fact one study of a village in the Midlands at this time clearly indicates that the stimulus for the unrest in 1607 was not the existence of enclosure itself, but rather the involvement of the land in commercial dealings – sale of the land to a London merchant led to its imbrication with war finance speculation and its treatment as a commercial asset in the negotiations that followed from this (L. A. Parker, 1949, pp. 57–9). The enclosure that took place here in the early seventeenth century was aimed at the racking up of rents for the purpose of paying the merchant's debts off; and though his income was subsequently doubled, he still went bankrupt.

Enclosure in the sixteenth century then, insofar as generalisations can be made for different areas, was principally aimed at an improved control over the land and its revenues, which brought with it the possibility of altering the use of land to suit changes in the market for various agricultural products. The regional aspect must be emphasised, for not all farming countries were equally suitable to sheep or cattle, let alone various arable crops. One shift that does seem to have taken place however was one which, during the seventeenth century, changed the Midland, predominantly clay, counties from arable to pasture farming, the production of grain shifting to the eastern counties with improvements in farming on light soils. The results of this can be seen today in the ridge and furrow landscape around Leicester and Northampton, where the pattern of previous arable tillage continues to show in fields long since devoted to pasture, in which there is no need to plough out the rise and fall of the ground to facilitiate the movement of farm machinery.

Enclosure in the eighteenth century on the other hand was primarily a response to the rising price of corn, as a result of which attempts were made to extend and consolidate cultivated areas capable of producting this crop. Commercial production of this crop in England in the later eighteenth century typically centred on the larger farms, while smaller holdings, as long as they retained grazing rights, could supplement their various vegetable and cereal products with dairy produce, using the manure on their own land as well. This pattern of existence has been shown by Ravensdale to have existed for a long period in Cambridgeshire fen-edge parishes, where the problems of effectively draining the fen ensured the continued existence of marginal lands until the coming of the steam-engine in the nineteenth century (Ravensdale, 1974, pp. 151–2).

A stimulation toward enclosure engendered by the rising price of corn therefore only moves those farmers (and their landlords where appropriate) who are in fact engaged in the cultivation of corn, or with farms deemed suitable for it. Small producers engaged in other lines of production are not affected by such stimuli – although they often come off the worse in reallocations of land by a landlord seeking to increase his rents. Where a distinction can be made between 'larger' and 'smaller' commerical farmers produing grain, a different problem arises, unrelated to the degree of enclosure: the fact that larger farmers, unlike smaller farmers, were not only immune from the effects of failures and short-term crisis but actually benefited from them. Admittedly the larger farmer would have a labour-bill to meet, but however poor the crop, he would always have a substantially greater marketable surplus than his smaller competitor, and was consequently in a position to benefit from the increased prices prevailing (Spufford, 1974, pp. 52–3).

The chronology and impact of the enclosure movement varied widely, and while trends have been broadly indicated for particularly regions (for example by Martin (1967) and Hunt (1957)), the differential nature of the phenomenon referred to as 'the enclosure movement' renders dubious any attempt to link it in a direct fashion with the process of social differentiation in the countryside. Certainly during the years between 1500 and 1800 what might be considered an English peasantry 'disappeared', but any examination of the issue shows that the reasons for this were quite diverse and certainly not reducible to the pace of enclosure. As we shall see below, the problem with the enclosure model is that it tends to emphasise a consciously directed programme of expropriation, whereas most modern accounts tend to support the conclusion that peasant proprietors were steadily eroded through a process of *appropriation*, that is, they were bought out by landlords (Habakkuk, 1965). Even this was not an entirely disadvantageous process, since some of those bought out could with the proceeds (providing that after settling outstanding debts there were proceeds) set up as tenant farmers, an instance that took place in the later eighteenth century in East Norfolk at least (Riches, 1937, p. 69).

The major thread of argument since the early 1950s has not been concerned with the rate of enclosure and the rate of social differentiation however: the 'radical' as opposed to the 'conservative' interpretations of rural history have instead fixed on the fate of the small landholder independent of the enclosure movement. There is of course some ambiguity in the definition of two such alternative views, since it is quite possible to subscribe to a 'disappearance of the peasantry' line and the same time argue that small farmers were a significant force at the close of the eighteenth century. Just as enclosure is not a universal and uniform tendency which everywhere had the same effects, there is no particular reason to regard small tenants or owner-occupiers in 1880 as being in general the descendents of smallholders of 1700, whether by 'descendants' is meant a class or kin filiation. Furthermore, the categories 'small' and 'large' farmer, like the term 'peasantry' itself, represent extremely vague ways of describing the outcome of distinctions arising on the basis of soil, weather, crops, family size, family property and market, to name but a few. In the early nineteenth century both the market gardener on the fringe of a large town and the Highlander on his coastal croft would both be classified as 'small farmers', but no-one would have supposed that this was anything more than a confusing coincidence. The debate about the 'small farmer' which continues today (Cooper, 1978, p. 24) turns on the question of the relevance of the treatment of eighteenth-century agriculture as 'capitalist'; the 'radicals' therefore argue that such a usage is both relevant and useful, while the 'conservatives' deny both these points.

Clearly such a discussion is central to this essay, but it is worth stating right away that those who in championing the existence, if not the cause, of the small farmer, seem to think that if small producers are to be found then this refutes Marx. This is of course a quite erroneous idea, assuming that Marx emphatically denied the possibility of capitalist relations existing in predominantly peasant economies – and ignoring the fact that Lenin devoted several years of his work to proving that capitalist relations were emerging among the Russian peasantry. Defenders of the 'small farmer' line also generally subscribe to a head-counting approach in their assessment of the structure of the rural economy – rather like treating as economic equivalents a man who owns a fleet of trucks and one who owns a wheelbarrow. The arguments of Chambers, Mingay and others can thus be shown to be misconceived and misdirected; but more important for the task in hand here, some of the evidence that they advance can be used to undermine their own arguments.

Mingay asserted quite confidently in 1962 that 'in 1800 England was in the main still a country of small farms' (p. 488), while recognising the growing importance of large tenant-farms and their contribution to the economy. One of the problems of this piece and the later essay on the small farmer (1968) is that no distinction is made initially between the small tenant-farmer and the small owner-occupier. This distinction is of course important for the arguments about the 'decline of the peasantry' in which 'peasantry' is assumed to involve independent owner-occupiers; but part of the problem derives from the lack of a range of means of distinguishing owners from tenants. Board of Agriculture Reports for the end of the eighteenth century made no such distinction, and the only means available to historians are the Land Tax returns, which did not however separate owner from tenant until 1780. Mingay has himself (1964) questioned the usefulness and accuracy of these returns, although evidence from at least one area suggests that his *a-priori* criticisms are without foundation (Martin, 1966). The problems of continuing to use the category 'small farmer' are substantial, although some clarification can be made presently.

The position of the small farmer at the end of the eighteenth century was according to Mingay as follows:

> That there was any disastrous decline of small farmers after the early eighteenth century is in fact improbable. The belief that a very great decline occurred in the later eighteenth century rests on an exaggerated view of the effects of enclosure and the technical advantages of large units; this was encouraged by contemporary writers, but is contradicted by the evidence now available. While it is still generally accepted that technical changes in farming (including the labour-inten-

> sive new rotations, the laying down of arable to leys or temporary grass, introduction of better and more extensive breeds of livestock, and the gradual adoption of machinery) were more readily adopted by farmers of capital than by small men, it is doubtful how far the economies of scale in agriculture were important before the middle nineteenth century. Further, the changes in the markets for agricultural produce do not point uniformly in the same direction. . . . In any event, the growth of larger farms was not fatal to small farmers, as the nineteenth century statistics confirm, and it is wrong to suppose that any sweeping or sudden change in farm sizes occurred, or was even possible in the conditions of the period. (Mingay, 1968, pp. 12-13)

Two problems arise in this argument that the small unit of production continued in importance during the period in question. The first concerns the use made by Mingay of 'economies of scale', as if the main difference between large and small enterprises was that of size or cultivated area. It has already been noted that the characterisation of enterprises by scale is nothing but a shorthand device which is used to denote a number of other features and conditions, and which by itself is devoid of great significance. But the way in which Mingay counterposes large and small here rests almost entirely on this device, since he supposes that the larger farms enjoy 'economies of scale' in their activities compared with those of the smaller farms. It is however entirely questionable that 'small' and 'large' farms seek to pursue similar objectives, whether from the point of view of market or crop farmed – typically the small farm of the later eighteenth century was more concerned with pigs, poultry and vegetables than larger farms, which were chiefly concerned with the production of grain for the market. Ironically, Mingay, by use of the term 'economy of scale' betrays an allegiance to a position that he appears to have refuted: namely that large agricultural enterprises have certain inherent advantages and that the index of development of an agrarian economy is the degree of domination of large units of production.

The second problem is related to this, for it involves the final remark that the growth of larger farms in the nineteenth century was 'not fatal' to smaller ones. The implicit criticism being made here is of a Marxist dogma according to which the development of capitalism in agriculture results in the increasing domination of large farms which eventually sweep away the smaller enterprises. Analogous refutations have been made of Marx's account of industrial development, and in either case the response is the same: that while certain remarks to this effect can be found in Marx's writing, it is in no way a central proposition, for the laws of motion of the capitalist mode of production that Marx outlined are not unilinear – for every tendency there is at least one counter-tendency, and the crisis-ridden development of capitalism periodically recasts the relations between enterprises in a variety of ways.

The point at issue is not whether the larger farms of the later eighteenth century were destined to erase smaller enterprises from the face of the countryside. The issue concerns how the changing relations between enterprises affected the viability of their activities. The alteration in farming regions is of relevance here, for clearly the development of a town would stimulate small producers (many of the products required, such as butter, cheese, poultry, bacon and so on could not be farmed on a large scale); while the same geographical change, combined with a slump in grain prices, might well lead to the dissolution of larger units into smaller ones. 'Market forces' could thus equally create small or large enterprises, depending on the conditions prevailing. As a corollary, the survival of small enterprises need not be a problem to be explained, nor can they be used to denote the non-capitalist nature of an economy in which they are the most numerous type of enterprise.

Another problem with the evidence that is used in such discussions, and a contributory factor to its air of indecisiveness, is that types of enterprise are asscssed (for the later eighteenth century) *via* individuals resident in specific parishes. An assumption is usually made quite implicitly that by 'farm' is meant 'consolidated unit of production', and that two types of individual relate to these: owner-occupiers, and tenants. These can again be differentiated by scale of activity, but this is not necessarily an accurate reflection of the type of farming characteristic of a region. The problem emerges in an article by Hunt on landownership in Leicestershire, where the category 'absentee landowner' is shown to include not only substantial holders of land, farmed by substantial tenants, but also small owners of land who are not at the same time resident in the parish. The manner in which the evidence is cast up, parish by parish, means that it cannot be ascertained where these small owners were resident – it could well be a neighbouring parish, for there is no reason why someone holding a few acres of land should hold them all in the same parish. The possibility arises then of small tenants in one parish being larger owners in another, or renting land in more than one parish and thus instead of being a small tenant perhaps being a medium one after all, farming an unconsolidated enterprise spread in at least two parishes. While inconvenient, it is not unlikely.

Hunt concludes that while there was an absolute decline in the number of small owners in his 44 parishes between 1790 and 1813, this decline was almost entirely accounted for by small absentee owners selling property when conditions were favourable. Small occupying owners actually increased in this period, although there was a decline again after the end of the Napoleonic Wars (Hunt, 1959, p. 505). Figures based on parish landholding are thus potentially misleading, and the problems that are indicated by Hunt are confirmed by evidence that Lavrovsky produced for 11 parishes in north-east Suffolk during the years 1797 and 1814. Lavrovsky, using an admittedly wide definition of 'peasant', suggests that such occupiers were the dominant holders of land in these parishes, but any problems that might arise from his nomenclature are nullified by the evidence that he produces concerning inter-leasing. He shows that of the 5554 acres owned by peasants in the old enclosures, only 2535 acres were owner-occupied, the remaining 3019 acres being leased out to tenant farmers. On the other hand, the peasants themselves rented 1331 acres (Lavrovsky, 1937, p. 189). The pattern that emerges is of a complex series of leasing arrangements, in which the pieces of land concerned are often no more than odd corners, and in all 73.1 per cent of tenants leased some land from the peasants. Despite the numerical preponderance of small owners in these parishes, a great deal of the land they in fact owned was not farmed by them (even if they occupied part of it), while just under half owned the equivalent of allotments, which could at the most only supplement an income deriving from wage labour. Much of this was perhaps the result of the structure of enclosure settlements and leasing arrangements which were merely temporary measures aimed at the redistribution of land for the purposes of consolidated farming; but such evidence does cast in doubt the viability of generalisation as to the 'decline' or 'survival' of the small producer, however defined.

The argument about enclosure and the decline of the peasantry refers itself to a dual process, the strands of which have been followed in some of the points raised above. The reason for the significance of the 'decline of the peasantry' is that it engenders a twin emergence: out of the decay of one set of rural relations are born both the rural proletariat and the capitalist farmers, tenants of the landlords. We have seen how this clear-cut schema for the emergence of the class relations of agrarian capitalism conceals more than it reveals. But the problems that arise when attempts are made to elaborate it beyond its most basic propositions should not lead one to think that it needs to be discarded; nor does the material presented above substantially alter the argument that the dominant relations in eighteenth-century agriculture were capitalist in the sense outlined in the introduction to this essay. There is however one strand of the argument that has so far not been directly discussed – the emergence of a rural proletariat. Again, problems arise here when historians suppose that this class is dispossessed in the most extreme sense, separated entirely from their means of production. Here again Marx is thought to be refuted when it can be shown that no such 'pure' proletatiat emerged during the eighteenth century; this has been argued most forcefully by Clapham, as will shortly be shown. But in fact this problem of the existence, or non-existence, of an agricultural proletariat has to be related to the above discussion of landholding and the size of enterprises.

It has already been shown that the complex pattern of landholding in the rural economy left substantial sections of the population without sufficient land to support their households. Wordie has questioned the manner in which Mingay describes holders of less than 20 acres as 'small farmers', since they are most likely to turn out to be labourers; and in any case the term 'farm' was rarely used in the eighteenth century of a holding of less than 20 acres. On the basis of data from the Leveson-Gower estates in Staffordshire and Shropshire, he concludes:

> The point about these very small tenants is, of course, that they were not farmers. They were for the most part industrial workers, drawing their main income from employment off

> the land in either the Ketley and Ironbridge areas of Shropshire or the coal mines and pottery towns near Trentham. The rest were agricultural labourers, working for the large tenant farmers. They had small gardens of a fraction of an acre, but were in no sense farmers themselves.
>
> (Wordie, 1974, pp. 601–2)

The significance of such evidence is that it both does away with the 'problem' of the survival of the small farmer, while at the same time showing that the existence of a body of wage labour for capitalist agriculture does not depend on identifying workers without any land at all. As has been argued elsewhere, Marxism is not committed to the dogma, so often ascribed to it, that dispossession is a condition for the formation of an agricultural proletariat (Hussain and Tribe, 1981 Vol. 2, Ch. 2). But even if it were, it can be shown that the arguments advanced by Clapham and Chambers and Mingay against the development of a rural proletariat are defective, and depend on an unwarranted use of certain statistics.

Clapham put forward the original thesis, according to which there was only a minor change in the proportion of labourers to farmers between 1688 and 1832, in an article published in 1923. Later in his *Economic History of Modern Britain* he qualified this original position somewhat, but it is convenient to begin by considering the earlier statement.

The dates selected by Clapham refer respectively to Gregory King's population estimate for 1688, and the Census returns for 1831, by which time enclosure was nearly complete, and while consolidation was to continue, the balance of the rural classes was defined in a way that was not to alter again until the twentieth century. Changing the order in which the figures are presented, they can be laid out as in Table 2.2.

Having presented the figures for 1831, Clapham concludes that 'here the ratio between labouring families and entrepreneur families is about 2.5:1' (p. 93). But this is only achieved by comparing all labouring families with all farming families, whether employing labour or not. In a previous discussion of the 1911 Census returns, which relate to persons and not families in employed classes, Clapham had noted that the possibility of a 'labouring family' containing more than one labourer meant that the ratio for families would be lower than that for persons;

but this is not reintroduced as a qualification when using the figures for 1831. But in addition to this, we have already seen that the classification of 'farmer' is a very inexact one – many of the 'family farms' for instance might not be big enough to support the entire household, leading to members contributing to the household economy through wages earned in outside employment. In addition, the seasonality of agricultural labour further complicates the scene, making certain estimates of the ratio of employer to employee difficult if not impossible.

The figures for 1831 are only qualified by Clapham according to regional variations in farming, and he quickly concludes that 'we have not a proletarian army under farming officers: all picturesque phraseology must be excluded. Numerically, the average agricultural unit must be compared, not with the factory, but with the handicraft workshop-master: journeyman or two: prentice or two' (pp. 93–4). In his book, as Saville pointed out in a discussion of these statistics (1969, pp. 256–7), Clapham did later compare employing families with labouring families while excluding non-employing families, an exercise which produces a figure nearer 5:1; and he also underlined the territorial

TABLE 2.2. Employed agricultural populations, 1688 and 1831

1688	*No. of families*	*Heads per family*	*income per family*
Freeholders	40,000	7	£84
Freeholders	140,000	5	£50
Farmers	150,000	5	£44
Labouring people and out-servants	364,000	3.5	£15
Cottagers and paupers	400,000	3.25	£6-10s.-0d.

Source: King, 1936, p. 31.

1831	
Families employed in agriculture	961,000
Entrepreneur families employing labour	144,600
Entrepreneur families employing no labour	130,500
Labouring families	686,000

Source: Clapham, 1923, p. 93.

dominance of the large farm in the early part of the nineteenth century (1926, p. 452) – unlike Chambers and Mingay in their *Agricultural Revolution 1750–1880*, who used the figures originally presented by Clapham to emphasise the dominance of *small* farms in the English landscape.

In any case, the immediate purpose of Clapham's argument was to show that there had been little change in the ratio of employer to employee during the eighteenth century, that is, that this century had not witnessed the formation of a rural proletariat. In dealing with the figures presented by King, Clapham again manipulates them in a manner which is unjustified, for he treats as 'farmers employing labour' both groups of freeholders and those designated as farmers, and treats 'labourers' as both labourers and cottagers. This artificially inflates the number of employees in the prevailing economy of the later eighteenth century, while at the same time inflating the number of those employing labour. At this time it was in fact more likely that 'family farming' on the part of freeholders would subsist a household for the same reason that 'cottagers' were likely to be independent – for at this time waste and commons still existed and would have permitted households to subsist off cultivated areas that would one hundred years later be too small. The ratio of labourers to farmers that Clapham derives is 1.74:1; and so, from the fact that the corresponding ratio for 1831 is only 25:1, he concludes that there had been only a very slow alteration in class relations in the eighteenth century, and that what alteration there had been was relatively minor. It would be more accurate to estimate the respective ratios at 1.9:1 and 5.3:1, and comparing these figures the conclusions of Clapham can be shown to be unjustified.

Such statistical evidence then that exists on a national scale points to the formation in the eighteenth century of a substantial class of agricultural wage-labourers. But as has been suggested above, this process was the outcome of a number of factors and cannot with accuracy be attributed to any one specific factor, like the enclosure movement (which in any case hardly counts as 'one factor' because of its heterogeneous nature). We have also seen that enclosure was identified as this master mechanism because it appeared to account for both the genesis of capitalist farms and the formation of a proletariat-in-general, driving surplus labour off the land and into the new towns to provide the basis of the urban labour force. The following section will show that this seriously underestimates the labour requirements of capitalist agriculture in the eighteenth century, but this section can be usefully concluded by considering the debate over enclosure and labour supply, since it resumes many of the varied issues raised in the preceding pages.

Marx identified enclosure as basically involving the *expropriation* of cultivators from their means of production, part of the history of the 'primitive accumulation' of capital which transformed means of subsistence and production into capital, and the immediate producers into wage-labourers. Dobb in his *Studies in the Development of Capitalism* closely followed the analysis of Marx and accordingly focused on the enclosure movement, but not to the exclusive degree to which Saville suggests in this passage:

> For Marx, and for Dobb, the growth of a proletariat was part of the historical process of primitive accumulation, and the emergence of the proletariat was mainly the product of the enclosure movement. Dobb, of course, was aware that a landless class could emerge from within a peasant community in ways other than by forcible expropriation, but although Dobb referred to Lavrovsky's evidence . . . and also at some length the Russian experience, it was the consequences of enclosure with which he was mostly concerned.
>
> (Saville, 1969, pp. 258–9)

Dobb's chapter entitled 'The Growth of the Proletariat' had actually placed some emphasis on the role of appropriation, rather than expropriation (1963, pp. 227–8) in which smallholders of land were simply bought out by larger owners. He also drew attention to the natural process of differentiation that always tends to take place in any community of rural smallholders, in which the poorer sections periodically relapse into debt and become dependent on the credits of larger owners. Spufford's more recent study of Cambridgeshire villages has also located this problem as a major source of differentiation, accumulations of debt eventually being liquidated by the transfer of land (Spufford, 1974, p. 80 fn. 48). Habakkuk too in his study of the disappearance of the English peasantry placed the emphasis on the process of buying out, a process made all the more invisible by the length of time that it took to radically alter the face of village landholding (Habakkuk, 1965, p. 655).

Chambers (1953) criticised Dobb's 'institutional' account of the formation of an agricultural proletariat by questioning the relevancy of enclosure to this process; and while he heavily qualified the terms of his criticism, and the conclusions that he drew, it is generally assumed by those influenced by Chamber's work that the major conclusion concerned the natural rather than institutional basis of an agricultural proletariat. 'Natural' is taken to mean that no specific mechanism other than a slow population growth is able to account for the appearance of wage-labourers, although there is of course nothing 'natural' about population growth in the sense that it is independent of social forces.

An earlier article by Chambers had sought to demonstrate that the later eighteenth century had not witnessed the demise of the small tenant and owner-occupier, which as we have seen is the other side of the argument over the disappearance of the peasantry. He concluded, on the basis of Land-Tax evidence drawn from Lindsey, Lincolnshire, that the multiplication of smallholdings was proof of the resilience of this type of farming (Chambers, 1947, p. 19). Tax was assessed at 1/- an acre, and Chambers points to the rapid development of holders of land in the 0–4/- group, that is, in the holders of less than four acres of land. According to the graphs that he presents, such holders totalled 20 in 1790, 70 in 1900, and 120 in 1820. No evidence is presented of any increase in total acreage occupied, and more recent work on the region shows that in fact there was little such increase, if total rentals are considered (Holderness, 1968, p. 322). As Holderness makes quite clear, these 'small owners' are in fact for the most part residents of cottages tied to particular estates, while not owned by them, and the majority of the working residents of such cottages were employed by bigger farmers as labourers (pp. 271–2). Chambers' early research into the small farmer shows, therefore, in the starkest terms possible, the manner in which a process of differentiation, in this case not unrelated to enclosure, promoted the rapid rise of proletarianised households, occupying small patches of land which by no stretch of the imagination could make them independent of outside employment. The agricultural proletariat, while hidden to some extent among 'owner-occupiers', was without any doubt substantially formed by the end of the eighteenth century. A number of factors contributed to this, among them varying forms of enclosure, but indebtedness and simple sale were also significant. Chambers in his criticism of Dobb sought, by questioning the basic mechanisms of proletarianisation, to discredit the characterisation of eighteenth-century agriculture as capitalist, in which large tenant farms were the clearest expressions of this type of economy. But while the mechanisms might be more complex, the outcome is not altered by such criticism, and as we have seen the figures advanced by Chambers and Mingay do not support the arguments that they then base on them. English agriculture in the later eighteenth century was dominated by tenant farmers who managed large consolidated farms. These farms were cultivated by wage-labourers who were at times required in great numbers. If Clapham were right in his figures for the ratio of farmers to labourers, agricultural production would have ceased long before 1832 for lack of labour. Those who argue for the small farm and the non-existence of substantial bodies of rural labour never seem to wonder where large capitalist farmers did find the labourers which they required in increasing numbers. This contradiction is never faced, however, since the actual organisation of such farms is rarely considered. The following section will do so, and begin to outline the features of capitalist agricultural production.

2.4 THE FARM AS CAPITALIST ENTERPRISE

> Under the existing conditions of English agriculture, it is almost invariably the fact that the landowner does not cultivate his land. He relieves himself of the responsibility of supervision, the risks of business, and the provision of moveable capital, by letting his land for a period, on terms, and subject to reservations agreed on, to a tenant, who provides such moveable capital more or less completely, and undertakes its cultivation. So fixed and invariable is this arrangement, that, even in cases where the landowner, either by choice or necessity, undertakes the occupation of his land, it is usual and desirable to place himself in the position of tenant, by separating the accounts, and charging himself with the amount of rent which might be obtainable if the land were let.
>
> (Squarey, 1878, p. 430)

This delineation of the proper functions of the landlord and the tenant in the management of the farm as a business enterprise appeared in the later nineteenth century, but the structure of responsibility and proper administration of a commercial asset is one that was forged in the eighteenth century. At the beginning of that century, estates were organised by stewards answerable to the landlord in a fashion not far removed from that typical of the middle ages; by the end of the century the administration of the estate was the province of a rising class of professional agents, vetting and regulating the activities of the tenants under their jurisdiction. Accordingly the conditions for retaining a tenant farm became more stringent, both in terms of managerial and agricultural skill and in terms of the profits that had to be made to stay in business. 'Progressive farming' became the model, and large tenant farms run by capitalist farmers the site on which it typically took place.

'Agricultural progress' used to be ascribed to the innovations of improving landlords, but research into the estates of eighteenth-century England has shown that the principal contribution of the landowner lay in the consolidation of farms, the maintenance of moderate rents, and the provision of secure tenure (Mingay, 1963, pp. 167–71; F. M. L. Thompson, 1963, Ch. 6). As far as the landlords were concerned their estates were a source of rental revenue, and while they naturally had an interest in increasing the yearly flow from their tenants, they had neither the time nor the knowledge to take anything more than a spasmodic interest in the technicalities of improvement. Apart from the odd exception (and in this case that popular 'improving landlord' Coke of Holkham is no such exception) the routine administration of the estate became the responsibility of land agents and bailiffs. This of course followed from the geographical dispersal of all but the smallest estates, and had been a common practice in medieval England when the lord was often absent from the main site of landholding. Such a steward was however charged simply with the maintenance of the economic stability of the estate, and the form of accounting between landlord and steward was directed solely at the detection of possible fraud on the part of the latter (Oschinsky, 1971, pp. 188–90).

As we shall see, this preoccupation persisted into the eighteenth century, but the changed conditions of landlord–tenant relations on the one hand, and the alterations in agricultural production on the other, meant that the administration of the estate as a mechanism for the production of revenue had also itself to change. For the landlord, the estate lands continued to function as his economic and political support, but for his agent the estate took on the appearance of a complex productive unit whose direction required professional skills and specific means of administration. The distance that this opened up between the conceptions of the estate on the part of landlord and agent respectively is expressed by the genesis of the first major textbook on estate management, Marshall's *On the Management of Landed Estates: A General Work; for the Use of Professional Men.* Published in 1806, it is in fact a shortened version of *On the Landed Property of England, an Elementary and Practical Treatise,* which Marshall had published in 1804 for landowners. This earlier book concerns itself both with practical matters and with the nature of property in general, considering among other things the factors entering into the value of an estate, and the manner in which they can be improved, only in the final section dealing with questions such as the terms of leases, the proper functions of managers and stewards and the proper assessment of rents. The later book, by the ommission of subjects 'intimately connected with the Landed Interest' is thereby transformed into an 'office book ... for the information and assistance of men of business' (p. xv). The function of the estate manager was thus not simply that of deputising for the landlord, but rather involved specific skills that were the consequence of training and experience.

Pollard has summarised the tasks of a typical agent in the eighteenth century as:

> setting of farms, drawing up leases, and tenancy agreements, seeing them observed, collecting rents, being the driving force behind the manorial court, if any, levying fines, 'riding the boundaries' in some districts, improving and supervising the home farm, keeping the estate accounts, including making payments to staffs, paying taxes, tithes and rates, watching poachers, and often supervising the household.
>
> (Pollard, 1965, p. 27)

This range of activities accumulated in the course of the century, bringing with it changes in methods of book-keeping, new forms of authority, and introducing the estate office as a central component in the administration of an estate. In the early part of the century, local rents were often simply collected by one of the tenants, while the estate was in the overall control of a respectable outsider, such as an attorney. The Leveson-Gower estates were for example controlled at this time by a cleric who introduced a decentralised system of under-agents for each property that was rare for the time. In addition to this, he sought to convert all leases from 'three lives' to 'at will', giving the agent greater control over the activities of the farmer and at the same time emphasising the importance of the agent (Wordie, 1967, pp. 55–9). Indeed, such was his zeal that holdings were left empty while suitable tenants at will were sought; although the consequence of at-will leasing, in abolishing fine income for the sake of a higher annual rental, led to pressure on the agent to abandon his policy.[4] After the death of this agent in 1720, however some of his innovations went into abeyance, and the political exile of the landlord resulted in his administering the estate direct for a period until 1742. In addition, the second Earl, who inherited in 1854, converted virtually the entire Shropshire estate back to leases for three lives combined with a very low entry fine, undermining the possibility of close control by an administrator. The development of estate management during the eighteenth century was thus not a simple story of the constant rise of new managers, although it was on the Leveson-Gower estates that James Loch, one of the most famous estate agents, rose to fame in the early nineteenth century.

One of the principal tasks of the agent was inscribed in the division of landlord's capital from tenant's capital, a division which was not constant and only rarely ran along the lines distinguishing fixed from working capital. Broadly speaking however, landlord's capital can be treated as the land, farm buildings, roads, cottages, fencing, water-supply and any improvements that resulted in more or less permanent improvements in productivity. Tenant's capital on the other hand can be treated as livestock, crops growing or in stock, implements and money in hand. Here then the role of the agent was to ensure the proper upkeep of the landlord's capital and to stimulate the improvement of the tenant's capital, which would in turn enable higher rents to be levied. The execution of this task required, however, suitable instruments, and in any case the actual nature of the landlord-tenant relation was quite varied, making generalisation difficult. For example, Holderness has enumerated nine possible types of relation, in which responsibility for the costs of maintenance of fixed and working capital devolve in differing degrees to landlord and tenant (Holderness, 1971, pp. 176-7). The basis of all such relations was however in general that the tenant hired land and buildings from a landlord, and with his own stock, seed, equipment and cash farmed the land. The payment to the landlord was a cash payment, made one or twice a year, specified in advance and not dependent on the size of the harvest. The variations in this relation principally concerned the responsibility for certain repairs, and the benefit resulting from any improvements. Expenditure on enclosure was invariably the province of the landlord, and any sitting tenant was charged for such improvement by an increase in rent.

In certain circumstances the long lease was employed as an instrument for the promotion of improvement (21 years in the case of Coke of Holkham (Parker, 1955, p. 158)), both as a guarantee of security for the tenant on his own improvements, and as a means for the landlord and his agent, through the insertion of husbandry and coursing covenants, to both promote good practice and protect the land against bad farming. From the point of view of the tenant, the importance of the long lease was that it guaranteed him the benefits of any improvement, and was an early substitute for the custom of tenant right that was to develop in the nineteenth century. Typical of such leases are those of Sir Harbottle Grimston, in which the landlord undertook to pay the Land Tax, and tenants were to make running repairs, for which they were allowed rough timber from the estate; the farm was not to be sub-let, no more than two consecutive crops were to be grown before a summer fallow, pasture or meadow was not to be ploughed up, and all dung was to be used on the farm (Clay, 1966, p. 54).

On any change in tenancy, two customs, that of hold-over and of pre-entry, safeguarded respectively the growing crops to the outgoing tenant while enabling the incoming tenant to sow crops for harvest in his first year of tenancy (Orwin, 1938, p. 148). Neither of these customs could however provide a safeguard against the tenant who let his farm run down towards the end of his tenancy, burdening the estate with repairs and maintenance necessary to put the farm in order before leasing it out again. The agent possessed no sanctions that could guard against such an eventuality, other than charging rentals sufficiently high to offset the costs of such expenditure – but then the competition for good tenants did not necessarily permit the additional of such a surcharge to rentals, which could not as a consequence be unilaterally raised in this way. This problem was circumvented in Lincolnshire by the custom of tenant right, which specified the rate of depreciation of different investments and improvements introduced by the tenant. In the 1840s, for example, the claying of lands was depreciated to zero over a period of four years, and since most leases in this area were yearly with six months' notice on either side, such arrangements provided secure compensation to outgoing tenants (Grigg, 1962a, p. 42). One of the major causes of neglect on the part of the tenant farmer was thus removed, but only in the later nineteenth century were such provisions formulated in Acts of Parliament; during the eighteenth century such security for the risks of innovation was provided by custom.

With the development of capitalist farming by the tenants of landed estates the administration of these estates became a complex task, involving the control of the tenancies as individual components of a larger unit of administration, while at the same time treating this unit as an economic entity whose performance had to be carefully monitored. As suggested above, this required the formulation of specific means of calculation, and it is important to consider these in their own right. But one of the main concerns in such calculation was the promotion of progressive and rational practice in farming, and the criteria employed involved questions of the 'model farmer' and the 'model farm'. While such models would naturally vary from region to region and from arable to pasture farms, there was general agreement among landlords that the 'model farm' was one of over 200 acres of consolidated fields, run by a tenant with £500 'capital' (cash and stock) who supervised a workforce of permanent and seasonal labourers.

Such enterprises were the subject of the farming tracts of the later eighteenth century, whose main concern was the good management of *farms*, rather than the proper activity of the good *husbandman*, a character to be found in the texts of the seventeenth century. The County Reports of the Board of Agriculture which date from the last decade of the eighteenth century are in many ways dedicated to propagandising on the part of capitalist farming through the recording and assessment of farming practice and the canonisation of exemplary big farmers. Thomas Robertson published in 1796 a summary of the Board Reports on this aspect, and in this can be found a clear description of the proper activities of the ideal farmer for the Board and Arthur Young:

> Farming is a liberal art, and consists in appointing and superintending labour; and in fact, it is less laborious to do a thing, than to tell others what to do, how to do, and to see it done. Were the farmer to hold his own plough, and perform the other menial exercises, he could not have time to make observations, to think, to read, to go to markets, to meet with his neighbours, to ride through the Parish and County, and neighbouring Counties, to see better practices, and get information from all quarters. Farming is the most difficult of all the arts, and nothing has retarded its advances so much as one farmer not knowing what another is doing at a distance from him; which accounts for the narrow prejudices among the professional men, and the aversion to everything that is good, if it be new. It by no means is here insinuated, that a farmer should be ignorant of what labour is; he should know how to hold a plough and drive a waggon, build a hay stack, and every other operation, and besides, perform them too, occasionally, upon every press of business.
>
> (Robertson, 1796, p. 54)

'Farming' is then quite distinct from 'husbanding' as the characterisation of agricultural activity, and while the organisation of the farm is thought in terms of the properties of the farmer – 'it is the farmer who gives the key to the whole' (Robertson, p. 52) – these properties are realised in terms of his supervision of agricultural labour, rather than its regular performance. The appropriate size of a farm is for instance considered by Robertson to be one that is related to the supervisory power of the farmer: if it is too large then he cannot control the enterprise effectively, while if it is too small he has time on his hands. Thus 'his time is equal to his business' (p. 53). It is not however suggested in this *Outline* that the landscape should be entirely dominated by large tenant farms; in fact a specific role is preserved for small farmers in that they provide services, such as carting, which are useful to the larger farmers (p. 64).

The conception of the tenant farmer as a supervisor is further emphasised in Young's *Farmer's Guide in Hiring and Stocking Farms,* where the first reason for the land of a farm lying in one consolidated block is stated to be that otherwise the farmer would not see the land so often, a dispersed farm being necessarily less well-adminstered than a unitary one (Young, 1770a, p. 16). Other works of Young, such as his *Rural Oeconomy* and *Farmer's Kalender,* are similarly dedicated to the elaboration of the proper tasks of the farmer and the good management of a farm, textbooks expressing contemporary assumptions and recommendations which, while not necessarily representative of agricultural practice in general, were themselves constitutive of conceptions of profitable farming and improvement.

These conceptions also found expression in the altered layout of the farmstead, which subsequent to consolidation and enclosure could be resited in the centre of fields which were worked. The preoccupation with manure typical of eighteenth-century farming (before the introduction of artificial fertilisers) made the construction of yards essential, and around these yards were arranged barns in which corn was threshed and livestock buildings in which straw and hay were processed into manure (Harvey, 1970, p. 77). The farmstead was also constructed in a manner that would afford the farmer as good a view of the working of the farm as possible, and this remained one of the major criteria of farm design even after the mechanisation of some processes altered the buildings into coverings for processes whose juxtaposition was dictated by the relation of those processes (Harvey, pp. 94–5).

But such a rational farmstead would only of course be found on the 'large farms' that were the model establishments sought after by landlords interested in rising rents. 'Improvement' and large tenant farms were synonymous, and such large farms were not only to be found on the light lands of East Anglia. In the early nineteenth century, for example, 56 per cent of the cultivated area of the Lilleshall section of the Leveson-Gower estates was occupied by farms of over 200 acres, while the average size of holding was 145 acres. At Trentham 28.9 per cent of the tenanted area was occupied by holdings of 100–200 acres, and

37.7 per cent occupied by holdings over 200 acres (Wordie, 1967, p. 331). Where there was a rise in the number of small tenancies there was no accompanying rise in cultivated area, and it seems likely that this rise only took place among tenants who were engaged in some kind of industrial employment. Furthermore, the attractiveness of the large holdings for prospective tenants was augmented on these estates by the fact that they were consolidated – evidence from maps indicates that Loch deliberately set about forming compact blocks of the fields belonging to any one holding, easing the work of the farm and the supervision of the farmer (Wordie, 1967, p. 352).

This throwing together and consolidation of holdings did not go unremarked or unopposed. What is interesting about the pamphlet literature however is that the criteria for a 'good farm' are similar to those noted above. Thus for example John Lewis' *Uniting and Monopolising Farms, Plainly Proved disadvantageous to the Land-Owners, and highly prejudical to the Public* advocates small farms on the grounds that average rents per acre for the landlord would be enhanced (because the average per acre on large farms was lower than on small farms), the small size of the farm made its working more convenient and efficient, and the employment of the family as labour enhanced the cheapness of such enterprises (Lewis, 1772, pp. 4–9). Other factors are advanced – such as the contention that the large farm depopulates the countryside, a conviction expressed also by Wimpey in his *Essay on the Present High Prices of Provisions* (1772, p. 38) and Forbes in *The Improvement of Waste Land* (1778, p. 159), who also suggests that the large farm is generally inefficient as a producing unit when compared with the small family farm. According to Forbes,

> The little farmers and their families do most of the work about the farm, very few day-labourers are necessary; and as the farmer constantly attends, directs and assists, in the business, he sees it is well done, and in the most frugal manner; whence it is easy to conceive, that the little farms are well cultivated, and no loss by waste land; for the little farmers are generally a most industrious set of men, and their families inured to frugality and close application to business; and hence they raise more provisions for sale, and cultivate their lands at a cheaper rate, then the great farmers, and therefore

> can afford to give a higher rent, or more per acre, than they who hire labourers to do all their work. (Forbes, 1778, p. 157)

It is clear from this picture of the small farm that one of the major advantages that it enjoys over the larger farm is the employment of family labour, which only has to be fed, not paid. Consequently the labour costs of such an enterprise are artificially reduced, and perhaps constitute the only means by which it can afford to pay a higher rent per acre. For what the defenders of the small farm at this time appeared to neglect was that the marketable surplus of such a farm was a smaller proportion of output than on a larger farm, assuming that it produced some crops that could be either consumed on the farm or sold at the market. It was true, as Kent complained in his revised *General View of the Agriculture of the County of Norfolk*, that the domination of local markets by large farmers and the resulting private dealing for most of the crop put small producers at a disadvantage (Kent, 1796, p. 134). As long as small producers met large producers in a common market place for the same product this would be almost inevitable, and small farms could only survive if they were prepared to adapt and concentrate on produce not available from large producers.

In Young's view however, the problem here was that small farmers were by the nature of their concerns relatively insulated from the agricultural advances of the day. As such the small farms of England represented an obstacle to the general improvement of agriculture, more or less impervious to the advice of the agricultural journalist and shackled by the family's over-exploited labour into a limited repertoire of techniques. Kent might refer to small farms as 'little hives of plenty' (1796, p. 133), but they were only 'schools of industry' (1775, p. 212) for the future wage labourers of the larger farms. As noted before, small enterprises in the vicinity of towns might possibily turn to market gardening or dairying, but those in more remote districts did not have such a choice. The lower rent per acre levied on large holdings was far from expressive of the relative inefficiency of such enterprises, rather it was indicative of the preference on the part of estate administration for substantial tenants who were prepared to innovate. The logic of the estate system then was also against the significant holding of land on the part of small farmers; which is of course distinct from stating that there were not many of them, rather it might be expected that they were actually quite numerous.

It is also important to note that the defence of small farming outlined by Forbes above assumes that small farmers are *tenant* farmers: the small:large opposition is not reducible to one of owner-occupier:tenant. The terms of the defence also assume that the smaller enterprises, like the larger, live from the sale of agricultural produce as commodities. The primary distinction of small from large then concerns the fact that the former work the farm with family labour, while the latter employ a permanent labour force; they might or might not be producing similar crops, but that is not here important. What must be emphasised is that this form of distinction between small and large enterprises is in no sense congruent with one between non-capitalist and capitalist forms of economic organisation. The presence or absence of wage labour is only indicative of the scale of the enterprise and the crops produced, not of the type of economy it represents. The small tenant farm based on the sale of animal and arable products for its survival as an enterprise must needs be organised capitalistically; that is, its resources have to be treated as commodities for sale or for the production of saleable goods; and in this respect, fields, cattle and the labour of members of the family are equal.

If agricultural resources are then treated in this way as commodities, it becomes possible to deal with the various factors entering into the production of agricultural commodities in a standardised fashion. The representation of agricultural processes in terms of monetary calculation becomes possible. Of course, there is much in agriculture that is clearly incalculable, and these factors are generally put down to Nature; but as Young suggested, much of the business of farming can be accounted for in terms of the wages of labour, since it represents 'that part of the expense which is *certain*' (Young, 1770b, p. xxv). Problems arise immediately of course, as Young proceeds to state, since such a formulation does not allow for the depreciation of equipment or the use of horses; but it does permit systematic comparison between farms employing labour in the production of similar outputs, or comparison year-by-year for one farm. The use of wages paid for different kinds of labour became the device which allowed Young and others to compare the productivity of different kinds of farm recorded either in

Tours or in the County Reports of the Board of Agriculture.

The wages of farm labour were not however the only factors to be entered into the calculation of the costs of farming, and in his *Farmer's Kalender* Young went on to summarise the headings and purpose of keeping accurate records for a farm:

> The grand object is to keep a ledger, or account for every article in the farm; in which an account should be opened for every field in the farm, or at least for every arable field, and one for all the grass. The farmer should in this book directly without the intervention of a waste-book or a journal, enter all his expenses; but, for doing this, he must take the trouble of dividing his rent to every field, so that the account may be complete, and not have an article for rent alone, unless it be a mere memorandum; and, before he balances his books at the end of the year, it is necessary for him first to cast up the sundry accounts, such as tythe–poor levy–various expences–and divide them in the same manner as rent.
>
> (Young, 1771, Introduction)

The purpose of the division by field is of course that otherwise such accounting would be useless; the fields represent sites of production with perhaps varying conditions, and their suitability for different crops can only be judged by the recording of costs, output, rent and so forth. Young's *Course of Experimental Husbandry* is for instance a detailed record of experiments over several years which seek to assess the productivity of different methods of cultivation with varying crops, and many of his other publications advising gentleman farmers are full of example after example of different 'ideal farms' complete with crops, labour costs and courses for appropriate fields.

The recommendations of Young should not however be read as indicative of the standard practice of improving tenant farmers; as late as 1858 an article in the *Journal of the Royal Agricultural Society* was deploring the haphazard records of English farmers, recommending that accounts should be drawn up annually and suggesting appropriate dates for this exercise (Coleman, 1858, p. 123). What is significant in the writings of Young is not that his advice should be representative of practice, but that it was in fact possible to represent the organisation of the farming enterprise in the way that he did. The tenant farmer hired land and buildings from a landlord in order to combine these with his own stock and wage-labour in the production of agricultural commodities. The cost of the hire of 'landlord's capital' was expressed in the rent of a farm, although the magnitude of the sum of money in fact handed over was determined by the prices prevailing for the commodities sold by the farmer and by the exact division of responsibility for repairs (outlined in the lease). Clearly the farmer had to have some idea of his costs, profits and other charges simply in order to estimate the limits of the rental negotiated with the landlord's agent.

Such farming account books that have survived from the eighteenth century indicate however that no regular profit-and-loss accounts were kept, records being limited to a description of the transactions arising from day-to-day farming (E. J. T. Collins, 1966). There was in this respect little change from two examples of seventeenth-century practice: the farming and account books of Henry Best for 1641, which simply list transactions which are themselves uncollated (1857); and the accounts of Robert Loder for the years 1610–20, which simply describe his farming practice without reference to financial transactions (Fussell, 1936). In the eighteenth century, the rotations used are recorded, the prices of materials bought in, the costs of stock, and the proceeds of sales follow each other in succession, with no attempt to utilise such records to evaluate the progress of the enterprise (Mercer, 1939).

It has been suggested above that the significance of Young's work on farm records was that he demonstrated what was possible, rather than what was actual farming practice; and in fact, while the farmer did require some basis of calculation for the assessment of prices, costs and rents, elaborate accounting procedures were quite redundant for such purposes. For in the eighteenth century, the process of production was organised in such a manner that direct physical comparisons could quite easily be made by the farmer. In a modern capitalist enterprise, accounts are used internally for the purpose of identification of regions of profit and loss in a standardised fashion, the financial year serving as a set period for year-on-year comparison. The drawing up of accounts serves to bring into a comparable form disparate circulation and production periods for the range of commodities produced, so that then the profitability of different operations can be compared.

In capitalist agricultural production in the eighteenth century these problems do not exist. The production process is a batch process, in which crops are in effect produced yearly at set times, and livestock has a similarly calculable cycle. The periods of production and circulation are fixed by the seasons; the annual product appears at regular and predictable intervals, in the case of crops as a physical quantity directly comparable with the crops of previous years. The sites of production are also discrete and fixed; each field can be identified as possessing a definite range of possibilities for different course of cultivation, and its contribution to the enterprise is estimable from the prices prevailing for the appropriate crops. The 'capital invested' on which a return is made is treated as the annually reserved stock of seed, whose return is expressed in terms of yield. These yields are subject to enhancement through 'good husbandry' and improvement, but they are in any case directly given and comparable. Costs in terms of labour hired can be assessed for each field, and combined with the cost of equipment owned and hired provides the possibility of calculating in a direct manner the viability of one particular enterprise.[5]

A comparison with the domestic manufactories of the eighteenth century, often run by merchants, demonstrates the unique position of the capitalist farm. Instead of all the capital invested being located within the bounds of the site of the enterprise, that of the manufactory is dispersed among a large number of workers engaged on processing the raw materials, and is also represented by completed but unsold stock still in their hands. Materials purchased by the manufacturer disappear into a production process that disgorges finished articles at irregular intervals, and there is no meaningful way of assessing the profitability of the enterprise at any particular moment in time. The periods of production are not successive, but intermingled, and it is consequently impossible to calculate a return on capital employed, since the nature of the category 'capital employed' is quite problematic.

The situation of the farmer is quite different. The work of the farm is organised in such a manner that direct physical comparisons can be made, from year to year, of labour costs, stock employed, yields and gains; and whereas the gains of a merchant are simply that, irregular advantages drawn from a succession of individual trading transactions, the 'gains' of a farmer are in fact equivalent to a profit on stock employed, since he cannot but estimate his gain as an annual return on stock and working capital employed (although there are deficiencies in this latter category). The regular intervals at which wages and rents are paid only serve to underline the comparability of the elements of the production process.

The farm, and not the estate, constitutes the capitalist agricultural enterprise of the eighteenth century, but the administration of the estate as outlined above did require that some means of accounting were employed. Unlike the farmer, the agent was in need of records that could be manipulated to produce results of one kind or another for the purpose of estimating the usefulness of enclosure and improvement or for the demonstration of the honesty of the agent. On most estates of the eighteenth century the master and steward system, developed in the Tudor period, was used to check against the possibility of embezzlement by the staff; further, it cast up the estate as a series of *units* (farms) rather than by different operations (capital invested, timber sold, produce sold) (Pollard, 1965. p. 272). As will shortly be shown, this placed severe limitations on the possibilities of such accounting.

Weber and Sombart's emphasis on accounting procedures as expressive of a capitalist rationality, focusing in particular on double-entry book-keeping, has, as Yamey points out, directed attention quite erroneously to the calculation of total profit; decisions concerning the commitment of resources can on the other hand only be made if the regions of profitability in an undertaking are know, and in such calculations the total profit on capital employed is quite irrelevant (Yamey, 1964, p. 119). The fact that estate accounts in the eighteenth century actually existed, as opposed to sophisticated farm accounts which quite clearly did not, should not lead to the conclusion that a 'greater degree of capitalist rationality' typified the estate compared with the farm. We have already seen that there were several factors not only inhibiting the development of farm accounting, but actually making it quite unimportant as a means of administration. The farm was nevertheless the unit of production, and the estate was simply an organisation which operated in some respects as a holding company, not engaged in production directly but rather supervising and in part financing the activities of subordinate enterprises.

The limitations of the methods employed to this end can be judged from the practices followed on the Coke estates in Norfolk, where an annual 'Audit account' was introduced in the early eighteenth century recording a final statement, year by year, of monies paid out and received by the estate, grouped according to the parishes concerned. The model used was the 'Charge and Discharge' account, where the agent charged himself for his receipts, and discharged himself according to his payments:

> The money due from each individual in each area was first recorded, and, together with the arrears due from the year before, it formed the 'Charge', the sum for which the agent must give account. There followed the 'Discharge' in which all items of expenditure for that area were noted. These items, added to arrears due at the closing of the books, together with the 'neat' or 'net' money (that is, the amount actually passed on by the agent as net income) balanced the 'Charge'.
> (R. A. C. Parker, 1975, p. 6)

The details for each estate were then summarised in an 'Abstract' which gave figures for old arrears, yearly rents, and casual profits on the 'Charge' account; and outrent paid, taxes, court-keeping expenses, bailiff's fees, repairs, improvements, deficiencies, 'neat money' and arrears remaining due on the 'Discharge' account. The agent is thus the pivot of this system of calculation, designed to demonstrate to his master that he has honestly acquitted himself of his responsibilties; but here detection of fraud is not the major objective of the different calculations, the system is used in the absence of other devices to represent the activities of the estate as a financial unit. The figures cast up are aggregates, but they do offer a general picture of the fortunes of the estate. The regions of profit and loss cannot be calculated, since the decomposition of the aggregated figures takes us back to individual parishes, and not to individual enterprises. But such data would presuppose that the farmers themselves could furnish some kind of information on which such enterprises could be constituted for the purposes of the accounts as economic agencies.

A series of texts in the eighteenth century recommended the adoption of the Charge and Discharge account for estate management, an early example of which is Laurence's *Duty of a*

Steward to his Lord (1727). This was replicated by Mordant (1761) and Lawrence (1768) who themselves offered no major modification to the schema on p. 88.

On the left hand side we have receipts, being either the rent of land organised by manor, or a series of occasional 'profits' which are in fact simply sums of cash from the sale of timber or the levying of fines. Payments are on the other hand distinguished by category, either for Land Tax, repairs to the manor house, servants' wages and so forth. While then it is possible to detect variations in payments under different heads from year to year, it is not possible from this Balance to assess the cause of variation in receipts. Of course, reference can be made to detailed sections of individual items, but in so doing the whole purpose of establishing an annual balance disappears, since this could in any case be done from the rent roll, for example. Not until the nineteenth century were specimen accounts published in textbooks which went beyond the model supplied by Laurence; but, as suggested above, this did not of itself create insurmountable problems of estate administration. The principal achievement of Charge and Discharge accounting was that combined with the new role of the estate agent in the eighteenth century it provided a form of representation of the estate as a single financial entity which could be managed as such.

An emphasis on the centrality of accounting procedures in the administration of capitalist enterprises is of course based on an assumption that improvement in the condition of the enterprise's rate of return is, other things being equal, a result of appropriate investment. The rate of profit is a return on capital invested; increase in the volume of profit results from an increase in the rate, or an increase in the amount of capital invested. The latter involves possible increases in scale of production, while such increases in agriculture are naturally circumscribed by the finitude of the land available at one time to any one enterprise. This might seem to place an emphasis on improvements in the rate of return, rather than in the addition of more units of capital, but both these operations appear to require some kind of monitoring procedure to identify the results of various measures introduced with the object of improving profitability. In either case, the kinds of financial controls available to the farm and estate might seem in such a situation to be obstacles to their efficient management.

In fact, the kinds of investment open to farm and estate in

An Abstract; or, an Accompt-Current ftated by way of Debtor and Creditor from all the 'foregoing Particulars, in order to shew the exact Balance:

From *Lady-day* 1725 to *Lady-day* 1726.

A. B. *Steward to His Grace the Duke of* K —, **Debtor.**	l.	s.	d.
REceiv'd the whole certain Rents from the four feveral Manors of *G, H, I, K*; as appears by the Rentals, *Page* 139	3525	7	5
REceiv'd the Cafual Profits of Courts by Fines, Hariots, and Surrenders, as appears by that Accompt *p.* 140, 141,	365	8	3
REceiv'd the Three Years Cafual Profits by the Tenants plowing up frefh Pafture-Land, as appears by the Accompt *p.* 142,	492	12	6
REceiv'd for the Sale of the Underwood, Timber-Trees, Heads, and Bark, in Prior's Wood in the Manor of *K.* as appears by that Accompt *p.* 143, 144, 145, 146	1738	5	10
Total of what I have receiv'd — *L.*	6121	14	0

per *Contra* — — — **Creditor.**	l.	s.	d.
PAid the four Quarterly Payments of the Land-Tax for the Manors of *G, H, I, K*; as appears by that Accompt, *Page* 148	131	0	0
PAid the 4 Quarterly Affeffments for the *Church, Poor,* and *Conftable,* for the Manor of *K,* Houfe, Park, and Gardens, and Woods kept in hand; as appears by the Accompt *p.* 148,	10	10	6
PAid the feveral Bills for the Repairs of the feveral Farm-houfes by agreement, as appears by that Accompt *p.* 149	154	0	0
PAid the feveral Bills for repairing and fitting up the Manor-Houfe againft the time your Grace comes down to look into your affairs; done by your Grace's Order, *p.* 150	187	5	0
PAid the feveral Bills for the Repairs and fitting up the Gardens, by your Grace's order, *p.* 151	184	6	0
PAid the feveral Bills for the feveral forts of Work done in the Park, as appears by thofe Accompts, *p.* 152	240	3	6
PAid the feveral Servants-wages, as appears by that Accompt and Vouchers, *p.* 153	192	10	0
Total Difburfements	1099	15	0
REturn'd and paid to *John Mead* Efq; your Grace's Banker, by feveral Bills, as will appear by his Accompt, to balance this whole years Accompt from *Lady-day* 1725 to *Lady-day* 1726,	5021	19	0
Total of what I have paid — *L.*	6121	14	0

This is a True Accompt, (Errors excepted) witnefs my Hand, *A.B.*

FIGURE 2.1. The debtor and creditor balance

Source: Edward Laurence, *The Duty of a Steward to his Lord*, London, 1727

the eighteenth century, apart from enclosure and consolidation, were relatively limited, and the practice of 'improvement' did not imply necessarily an increase in capital investment. Much of the increase in the productivity of the consolidated farm came from the application of 'good husbandry' under the effective supervision of the farmer. Changes in crop rotations, and improvements in livestock, both of which have been identified as typical means for the increase of output in the period (F. M. L. Thompson, 1968, pp. 63–5), did not require large outlays, although it must be admitted that the cost of enclosure rose significantly through the century (Martin, 1967, p. 131).

There are grounds however for doubting the wisdom of treating enclosure automatically as if it signifies a major investment likely to yield increased returns in its own right. Holderness has for instance shown that out of the six million acres of parliamentary enclosure in the period 1740–1840 well over four million acres consisted of land already cultivated and at least relatively productive (Holderness, 1971, p. 165). Figures for East Anglian rentals over the period 1746–1870 also show that a sharp upward turn only takes place in the expenditure on repairs and improvements in the period 1806–10, having fluctuated between £2438 and £6487 in the preceding fifty years (Holderness, 1972a, p. 439). Expenditure on the Coke estate fluctuated in a similar manner; where the outlay in repairs and improvements expressed as a percentage of rental was around 10 per cent in the example just cited, it was slightly higher on the Coke estates, varying from 14 per cent in 1786–95, to 19 per cent in 1796–1805, falling again to 13 per cent in the years 1806–15 (Parker, 1975, p. 94). In each of these cases, the figures for investment include not only the replacement or improvement of existing capital stock, but also its repair and maintenance; but even with the consequent inflation of statistics on agricultural investment, the amount laid out by even some of the most progressive eighteenth-century landlords is far below the 27 per cent of rental which Thompson calculated as a norm for the later nineteenth century (R. J. Thompson, 1907).

East Anglia was the most progressive region of agricultural England in the later eighteenth century, and the farming practice of its advanced areas is often associated with progressive farming *tout court.* Its main significance however, symbolised by the turnip grown on its light lands, was the solution of the problem of winter feed, enabling a farm to graze a larger amount of livestock during the course of the year and then during the difficult winter months feeding them on fodder crops grown on the farm. This in turn increased the amount of manure available for use on the arable fields, and so the farm established a new cycle of interdependence of its elements at a higher level of productivity. The cropping patterns associated with this 'new husbandry' were however not transferable to the heavier clay soils of the Midlands, where adoption of similar courses would have involved extensive draining and fertilising, which would have eroded any additional profit to be gained from such a system. Improving tenants in the Midlands often found themselves in a cleft stick.

> On improving estates where attempts were made to reduce the corn acreage and expand stock farming, the inability to grow fodder on the arable imposed a limitation on the clayland farmer. Because the grassland was forced to provide both winter provender and summer grazing for stock, a constant clash arose over the use to which the grassland should be put. If the same head of stock was to be carried throughout the year, a large part of the grass acreage was locked up as meadowland during the summer, which was the period of greatest activity in grassland livestock farming, with spring calving, summer milk from the dairy herd, and summer fattening off grass. The Leicestershire graziers had long accepted the low profits per animal involved in buying in the spring and selling in the autumn as the price of carrying large numbers of stock on the summer pastures. But Gloucestershire farmers were forced to keep small dairy herds throughout the year because of the small hay supplies and the low yield of their pastures.
>
> (Sturgess, 1966, p. 107)

Without substantial investment, which would only be reflected in high rents, claylands could not compete with Norfolk farming, where complicated rotations could eliminate the bare fallow and permanent pasture, in effect extending the amount of land available for farming. So long as lighter lands produced grain under unchanged conditions other regions were unable to compete without increasing their costs of production so much that little or no profit resulted from concentration on grain.

Midland clay areas, previously centres for the production of wheat, had in the face of such competition to concentrate on livestock. A fall in the price of grain after 1815 made it even more difficult for such areas to re-enter the grain market without intensive investment, and while there was a shift during the 1820s to malting barley and wool as profitable commodities in the markets, it was again light lands which had an advantage in their production (Grigg, 1962b, pp. 98–9). By this time however Norfolk farming had lost some of its pre-eminence to the East Lothians, consequent on the heavy labour requirements of turnip husbandry and the incidence of diseases which proved hard to eradicate (Jones, 1962, pp. 146–7); the cheapening of oil-cake, bought in on the Midland farm as fodder, and the greater availability of cheap clay-pipe drainage, at the same time moderated the advantages previously enjoyed by light lands. An altered price structure made investment in drainage and fertiliser in certain clay areas an economic proposition, and it was this which was to stimulate the higher rates of investment typical of nineteenth-century agriculture.

The conflicting pattern of 'progress' can also be charted through the increasingly complex patterns of labour requirements that innovation brought into the farming cycle. Not only did the new husbandry introduce an altered pattern of seasonal demand for labour, it required a higher input of labour per acre than the old system; and so far from being a major cause of rural depopulation, the new farming methods increased the total labour force needed to run the farms on which they were practised. In addition to this, accepting an increase in yields of the optimistic order of 50 per cent, the increase in output per worker was virtually nil, such that as Timmer and others before him have emphasised, 'the English Agricultural Revolution increased land, not labour, productivity' (1969, p. 392). Increasingly complex rotations of corn, root and leguminous crops produced overlapping work schedules and demands for summer labour, increasing the demand and at the same time reducing the period in which it was needed. Rapid and convergent crop-ripening over a wide area disrupted the old pattern of migratory labour which depended upon the differential timing of ripening between upland and lowland, heavy land and light land (E. J. T. Collins, 1969, p. 62)

This situation made the harvest period a critical one for many large farms, and the first response was to replace the sickle with the scythe, first for spring grains and then for the bread grains, wheat and rye (E. J. T. Collins, 1969, p. 82). This had a 'labour-saving' potential of around 45–50 per cent over earlier methods, but the greater rate of cutting made possible also altered the organisation of the field workers employed to bind and stack. Here again, increases in productivity followed from a reorganisation of farmwork on the basis of established techniques and not by the increase in capital laid out. The threshing machine for example, the first practical item of farm machinery, could not be immediately adopted by a farmer faced with a labour shortage unless he could command the labour necessary to gather his harvest in the first place. The thresher, when it came, displaced the winter work of permanent labourers, not the harvest work of seasonal employees (Harwood Long, 1963, p. 19).

The position becomes clearer if Figures 2.2 and 2.3, taken from Timmer's article on labour requirements, are considered. Two hypothetical model farms of 500 acres each are considered, constructed on figures supplied by Young's *Farmer's Kalender*; they are presumed to share the same Norfolk soil, differing only in that the cropping system of the new farm includes turnips and clover. Livestock is homogenised into animal units of standard appetites, and other assumptions are made in the course of calculating the output of different crops and their relation to the number of animal units that can be supported for the whole year. The important conclusion from the argument that Timmer presents is that the new farm requires 21 full-time labourers, while the old requires only 15. As can be seen from Figure 2.3, the seasonal labourer requirement for the new farm both fluctuates more widely than that of the old, and has two peaks per year instead of one. The June peak for example, caused by the need for mowers, and the ploughing and sowing of turnips, created a demand for 24.5 seasonal workers according to Timmer's calculations, while on the old farm this was a slack month.

With the ruralisation of the agricultural economy, the gradual destruction of cottage industries and the altered patterns of seasonal labour, farmers found an abundant supply of casual labour increasing hard to find, even by offering increased wages. This situation was one of the conditions for the eclipse of Norfolk farming, changing patterns of migration starving it of the manpower necessary to run its labour intensive courses. The

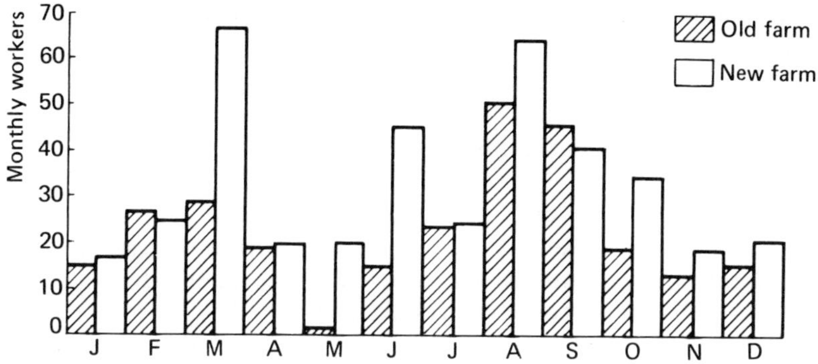

FIGURE 2.2. Monthly labour units on 'new' and 'old' farms

Source: Timmer (1969) p. 393

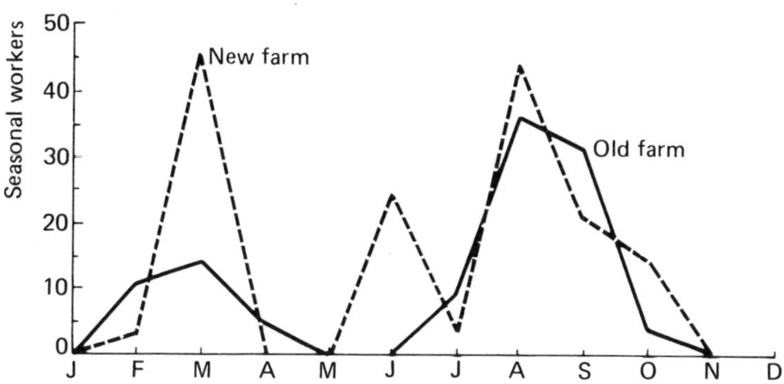

FIGURE 2.3. Seasonal labour requirements on 'new' and 'old' farms

Source: Timmer (1969) p. 394

emergence of 'closed' parishes of controlled estate labour became conditional on the existence of 'open' parishes in which casual and irregular labour resided often at some distance from their places of employment, contributing also the 'gangs' of women and child labourers that the Norfolk system eventually came to reply upon (Holderness, 1972b, p. 127). Not until later innovations in the production and processing of wheat were available would it be possible for Norfolk to overcome the problems of labour shortage created by its own methods of farming, and assume again a dominance in the national production of grain.

It has been argued in this section that the tenant farm of the eighteenth century was a capitalist enterprise in which factors entering into its production process were calculable and organised according to the most effective disposition of resources for the creation of profit. It was unusual however for the capitalist aspects of the farm to be expressed in terms of heavy investment; in the conditions prevailing in the eighteenth century, the effective disposition of established techniques and practices was one of the major means of increasing output. Where significant changes were made, such as in Norfolk, this did not involve outlay of capital, rather the change of course and the purchase of more livestock. It was in fact the low capital costs of Norfolk farming that made it impossible for Midland farms to compete until the nineteenth century brought altered conditions, and made the heavy investment in fertiliser and drainage an economic proposition. Changes in farming practice were of course also consequent on alterations in the structure of the various markets related to farming, and some comments on this aspect of the eighteenth-century agrarian economy can perhaps be made in closing.

2.5 THE FORMATION OF THE HOME MARKET

'The market' is often treated, by historians and economists alike, as if it were a simple consequence of the exchange of goods for money, a mysterious but pervasive force which polices the economy independently of the volition of economic agents. Commerce and the rise of the market are treated as synonymous with the rise of capitalism, and explicable quite simply in these terms. Conceived as the means for the 'allocation of scarce resources', it is in fact a mechanism which consitutes these resources as 'scarce', so that this popular economist's formula is little more than tautology. Indeed, what is usually referred to as 'the market' is no more than a blank space occupied by a diversity of changing relations – hence the mystery of 'market forces', so long as these are conceived in terms of an origin in this blank space. For in order to understand the manner in which capitalist enterprises are linked, wage levels and other costs determined, and a price structure for produce developed, an understanding of the different relations producing these is required, without assuming that the formation of say, a national market in wheat, is simply a matter of geographically aggregating localised exchanges. The account below does not seek to provide a general picture of these relations, nor does it consider the growing impact of foreign trade and its conditions; instead it is confined to some remarks on the nature of the 'home market' for agricultural produce in the eighteenth century which can be related to some of the points raised in the preceding pages.

It is perhaps convenient to begin with the geography of distribution of commodities in this period, since the means of distribution and the direction of flows underwent consistent modification. The emergence of large urban consuming centres, particularly London, coincided with a shift from rye to wheat as the staple bread grain, stimulating the production of wheat in regions with access to London. Such access for bulk transport of grain was primarily waterborne; the regional road network did not facilitate the overland transport of grain and other farm produce, and river traffic, linked to the coasting trade, accounted for the movement of crops over any significant distance. It has been claimed that in the seventeenth century water transport was twenty times as cheap as wheeled carriage over comparable distances (Willan, 1938, p. xii), and of course in England no inland site was ever a great distance from the sea or coastal port, unlike in Continental Europe. The development of East Anglia as a major source of grain for London is only explicable in this way, since neither river nor road transport would have sufficed to move grain from Norfolk to London – the rivers flow the wrong way, and the distances by road would have been prohibitive. Waterborne traffic did however have its own problems: rivers were subject to flooding and drought, and their increasing use for water-wheels, weirs, dams and mills conflicted with their use for trade (Willan, 1936, pp. 21–3), while seaborne trade was vulnerable to storms and wars. Although it has been suggested that the better records surviving for seaborne trade might have let to its overestimation compared with roads as a means of transport (Everitt, 1968, p. 58), it can be assumed that not until the later part of the century, with the development of canals and turnpike roads, did the advantages of waterborne transport for bulk cargoes begin to diminish.

The improvement of the road system centred around London, by 1750 most of the main roads between London and the provincial centres having been turnpiked together with some major inter-provincial routes. By the mid 1770s a relatively comprehensive road network had been developed (Albert, 1970, pp. 188–9), but the contrast between such main roads and the lanes and tracks of rural England is indicated by Cobbett's need for guides and directions to traverse the maze of parish-based bye-lanes once off the turnpike (Cobbett, 1967, p. 31). While travel between regional centres was greatly improved by the construction of turnpike roads, local travel remained problematic; and this led to the somewhat paradoxical situation that the supply of goods, including locally produced agricultural goods, to rural areas created more problems than the provisioning of large towns. Large numbers of small market towns remained necessary primarily as centres of distribution to an immediate locality rather than as means for the transmission of crops to merchants, or as centres of consumption (Everitt, 1968, p. 60).

This last point is related to the fact that during the eighteenth century markets and fairs declined in importance for the distribution of agricultural produce. Instead of the farmer carting his produce to market and selling it off to the highest bidder or piecemeal in a public sale, the practice of selling whole crops by sample to merchants in private became established. Such negotiations took place in inns, and resulted in the public market place becoming of quite secondary significance in the marketing of agricultural produce. The documentation of such transactions is of course virtually non-existent, since it relied on verbal agreements; but the rising importance of the inn during this period perhaps indicates the degree to which the structure of trading altered (Chartres, 1973, pp. 67–9).

In part at least these changes were related to the alteration of Corn Law legislation in 1660 from protection of the consumer to protection of the producer, postively encouraging export and permitting imports only above a fixed price level in the home market. This stimulated the production of grain and provoked fierce arguments over the effects that such legislation had on the economy as a whole, in which the interests of landlords and manufacturers apparently conflicted. Poor crops after 1756, and a fall in exports after 1765, meant however that in the critical period of development of the agrarian economy the legislation in force was ineffective (Barnes, 1930, p. 31) – and after 1792 Britain became a permanent net importer of grains, the control of the home market depending on the degree to which foreign grain could be excluded.

During the eighteenth century a more or less uniform price trend for grains was established, although Thorold Rogers in his *History of Agriculture and Prices* identified six distinct price regions in England at the beginning of the century (John, 1968, pp. 238-9). More recent work has questioned the degree of autonomy that this gives to regional centres in price formation (Granger and Elliot, 1967, p. 258), and their examination of the trends in the rate of change of prices does indicate that a similar set of forces was operating on bulk traded grain over a wide geographical area at this time. Gilboy has however noted that this uniformity was completely unrelated to the trends in wages, which in three principal regions both altered at different rates and stood at different levels (Gilboy, 1934, p. 219). The formation of a national market in grains which was more or less uniform in price neither engendered nor was related to a similar trend in wage levels, despite these being largely subsistence payments.

The nature and structure of the national market in grains is illuminated by the incidence of popular protest during the eighteenth and early nineteenth century which was both expressive of the changing conditions of agriculture and of seasonal fluctuations. For the pattern of disturbance in times of grain shortage was distributed over the year in a similar fashion to the pattern of rural recreational activities, punctuating the succession of activities in field and barn (Malcolmson, 1973, p. 14). Disturbances during the eighteenth century were for example usually clustered around two phases of the agricultural year: the period, following the harvest, during which the crop moved through the distribution system, and between Lady Day and Michaelmas, when prices were at their highest following a poor harvest, and exports were the object of discontent. Shelton for example has identified the importance of movements of grain towards ports in the West Country disturbances of 1766 (Shelton, 1973, pp. 24–6). 'Food riots' during this period were then directly related to the distribution and marketing of grain, while the mechanisms which effected this were at the same time becoming concealed from public supervision. It is clear for instance that the popular 'price-fixing riot' studied by E. P. Thompson had an ephemeral existence between the altered Corn Law legislation of the seventeenth century and the rise of selling by sample and bulk dealing which rendered the market places of small towns steadily more peripheral to the national market (Thompson, 1971, p. 108).

Rose has identified the first of these 'price fixing riots' as taking place in Oxford during April 1693, shortly after the legislation of 1660 had come into effective operation with the poor harvest of the 90s. This made the actual incidence of the new measures apparent to the consumers of grain, and set a pattern for the eighteenth century (Rose, 1961, pp. 281–2). Those disturbances studied by Thompson were primarily those sited on small rural markets, the participants being rural labourers and artisans from villages and small market towns. As noted above, given the structure of the transport network, this implies that the grain over which such disturbances occurred was primarily that which was earmarked for supply to local consumers, that is, the rioters, since the supplies directed towards larger towns would not have physically appeared in the market place. Later in the century contract workmen displaced such local residents as the dominant force in disturbances, since their position in the countryside made them vulnerable to any shortages that might arise (Stevenson, 1974, pp. 49–50).

The personnel of such 'riots' shifted during the course of the century from local residents associated with agricultural production, to wage-labour employed in the countryside for short terms. By the end of the century, agricultural labour was already turning away from popular protest in the market place oriented principally against merchants and the mode of circulation of agricultural products, and adopting instead a practice which has been termed 'collective bargaining by riot', aimed at farmers as employers, linking demands for a reduction in prices with demands for higher wages. As an agricultural proletariat became more established, the capitalist farmer, rather than the merchant, became the object of agitation.

This shift brought with it different forms of protest. The sequestration and distribution at a 'just price' of a load of grain was of course no longer possible; instead incendiarism and machine breaking became the sign of rural discontent. The first major sustained outbreak, the Swing disturbances of 1830–31, represented the initiation of widespread conflict between capital and labour in the countryside which was conducted in many ways like a modern trade dispute (Hobsbawm and Rudé, 1973, Appendix IV). The Hammonds described this as the 'last labourers' revolt', as if the tide of disturbances that spread slowly around Southern England was the last effort of a fading social force, the end of a line stretching back through the centuries to Ket and Wat Tyler. Rural protest does not possess such a trans-historical presence however; it arises on specific grounds for particular reasons, and as has been indicated briefly above, changes as to purpose, conditions and membership over relatively short periods. Far from being the last labourers' revolt in a dying tradition, the Swing disturbances emphatically announced the new conditions of rural organisation and displayed the new patterns of activity that were created to meet them.

The altering rhythms of rural protest are thus related to the changing structure of the agrarian economy, and can in part be used as indices of such change. The 'rise of capitalism' or the 'penetration of market relations' might be used to summarise such changes, but without considerable elaboration such conceptions prove more of an obstacle to analysis than anything else. Once such elaboration has taken place, such terms are both redundant and pitifully insufficient, being revealed for the teleological and rhetorical devices thay they are.

The purpose of this essay has been to elucidate the nature of the agrarian structure that Marx referred to as the classical model for the development of capitalism. It was necessary in so doing to indicate some of the problems with contemporary accounts of eighteenth-century English agriculture, but the dominant concern remained even here the investigation and elaboration of capitalist agrarian organisation as it was developed in England. It must be emphasised that this structure is no more than a 'model' – an exemplar, not an essential form or even an original form. The structure of enterprise relations for instance was in England indelibly stamped with the form of landholding and property that had developed; and the existence of the large tenant farm as the 'typical' capitalist enterprise should not lead to the conclusion that such tenurial relations are somehow a precondition for capitalist farming. A closer involvement on the part of the landlord in the running of the enterprise, or even the assumption of the direction of the enterprise by the estate itself as in East Prussia, is sometimes thought of as an imperfect application of a pure and prior capitalist model, explicable by the survivals of feudalism or traditionalism. It is along these lines that the pre-Revolutionary development of Russian agriculture is commonly discussed, often obscuring quite specific conditions under the weight of a comparative method in which diverse instances of capitalist economic organisation are organised into hierarchies of 'routes to modernity'.

The 'English model' provided here is not intended to be the source of such a typology. Instead, the object has been to discuss, on the basis of relatively abundant secondary material, the manner in which capitalist relations developed in eighteenth-century English agriculture, so that a better appreciation can be gained of the heterogeneity and variations of this form of economic organisation that are possible in agriculture, in which it is sometimes assumed that capitalist organisation is an unnatural and external imposition.

3 'Industrialisation' as a Historical Category

When Engels sought in 1845 to summarise the emergence of the English working class, he began as follows:

> The history of the working class in England begins in the second half of the last century, with the invention of the steam-engine and of machinery for working cotton. These inventions gave rise, as is well known, to an industrial revolution, a revolution which altered the whole of bourgeois society; one whose world-historical significance is only now beginning to be recognised. (Engels, 1969, p. 37, amended)

The casual manner in which the term 'industrial revolution' is introduced here, as if it were common parlance, is counterpointed by the statement that only recently had the revolution been recognised for what it was – some eighty years after its inception, according to Engels' chronology. And in fact, Engels' use of the term 'Industrial Revolution' here is far from repeating common usage, in German (the book was originally published in Leipzig) or in English. The term had been used in Adolphe Blanqui's *Histoire de l'économie politique en Europe*, where the industrial revolution is described as 'taking possession' of England in a manner reminiscent of the French revolution (1837, Vol. 2, p. 209) but there is no reason to suppose that Engels had read this book, and it was only translated into English in the 1880s. In some respects then, it is possible to say that the phrase which Engels passes off as 'well known' represents the first usage in an English context[1].

This would be a relatively minor point if it were not for the rider that is added to the statement above, a rider which seems at first quite paradoxical. If it were common knowledge in 1844–45 that England had in the later eighteenth century experienced an industrial revolution, why did this momentous event go unrecognised for decades? Everyone knew about the French revolution; why should it take until 1837 for the metaphor of revolution to be applied to the English economy? The delay is important, for many recent accounts of culture and politics in the late eighteenth century assume that those living through the period identified as the 'Industrial Revolution' were aware of its existence as such and were duly affected by it.

It would be wrong of course to suppose that the absence of a certain formula is evidence of its virtual non-existence as a conception; and if we look at some of the economic literature of the early nineteenth century it is possible to trace a set of factors and a periodisation that were later used by Engels to identify the content of the term 'Industrial Revolution'. Cayley for instance in his book *On Commercial Economy* discusses the consequence of the increased use of machinery on labourers in terms of the improvements in the cotton industry since 1760, referring to an article in the *Edinburgh Review* as a source (Cayley, 1830, pp. 2–4). Gaskell in *The Manufacturing Population of England* also identified 1760 as a turning point, prior to which manufacture was directed to a domestic market (1833, pp. 15–16). Other writings appearing in the later 1820s provided a similar analysis; but the earliest usage of this chronology that Clark can find in his survey of the subject is to be found in Galt's *Annals of the Parish* of 1821, referring to an increase in the population following the 'mechanical inventions which introduced the cotton trade into this country, and to the cultivation of the cotton tree in America' (Clark, 1970, p. 9)[2].

In England then it is possible to find examples of accounts tracing the recent development of the economy from 1760 – and the uniformity of the chronology and description in these writings of the 1820s is itself very striking. Nef has pointed out that 1760 possesses a more orthodox historical significance, namely the accession of George III; and he goes on to suggest that the uniformity of an economic periodisation which takes 1760 as a point of departure is partly derivative of a transcribed political history (Nef, 1943, p. 2). While there is some truth in this contention, it must be noted that this periodisation involves not merely conventional historical epochs, but historically specific artefacts: namely the spinning jenny and the steam engine – machine and power source respectively. But none of these texts use the term 'Industrial Revolution' to summarise the descriptions which they provide. In France, where the metaphor of revolution was more readily applied, instances can be found of the conjunction of 'industry' and 'revolution' in 1827, or even in much looser form in 1806, but such usage was unrelated to the kind of economic writings current in England during the 1820s which employed the idea, if not the word (Bezanson, 1922, pp. 344, 346).

Blanqui's book, combining an economic history of European development with the exposition of economic theories relating to this process, does as mentioned above clearly draw on the French Revolution for a metaphor of catastrophic social change, but unlike the French writings of the 1820s it attaches a specific set of elements and their effects to this novel term, the 'industrial revolution':

> Just as the French revolution witnessed great social experiences of earth-shaking proportions, England began to undergo the same process on the terrain of industry. The end of the eighteenth century was signalled by admirable discoveries which were destined to change the face of the world and increase in an unforseen manner the power of their inventors. The conditions of labour underwent the most profound alteration since the origin of societies. Two machines, henceforth immortal, the steam-engine and the spinning machine, overthrew the old commercial system and gave birth almost at the same moment to material goods and social questions unknown to our fathers. (Blanqui, 1837 Vol. 2, pp. 207–8)

Thus at the moment that the 'industrial revolution' enters the public realm it becomes associated with specific mechanical inventions and their effects. But as we shall in a moment see in the case of Engels, this early usage coupled the 'industrial revolution' directly to problems of social domination – Blanqui goes on to discuss the new order of factory worker and capitalist as an 'industrial feudality' in which the worker was a 'new serf of the workshop' (p. 208). The apparent technicism of a means of economic periodisation conceals a concern with questions of power and domination not conventionally associated with present-day economic histories of the industrial revolution.

Engels then used a novel term to describe a set of events beginning eighty years previously which had only been discussed as such for fifteen or twenty years. These disjunctions will be elaborated and explained later, but for the moment it is worth considering the manner in which Engels described this 'Industrial Revolution'.

'Before the introduction of machinery, the spinning and weaving of raw materials was carried on in the workingman's home' states Engels, beginning his account of the period of rural domesticity, in which the restriction to the home market limited output and competition (Engels, 1969, p. 37). This rural scene of tranquillity, stagnation and servility was rudely shattered by a wave of gadgets: first came Hargreaves' jenny in 1764, raising the output of yarn and making possible the employment of more weavers, the farming weaver abandoning farming for the higher rewards of wage labour, while spinning became concentrated first in whole families, then in mills set up by the manufacturer. The factory system had been initiated, and received a fresh boost with the invention of the spinning throstle by Arkwright in 1767, a barber living in Preston (Engels, 1969, p. 41). Crompton combined the peculiarities of the jenny and the throstle into his mule in 1785, and with other inventions related to the preparation of cotton, the spinning of cotton became a factory-based process. By the early years of the nineteenth century a power loom had been developed to such an extent that it could begin to displace weavers, up to this time enjoying the benefits of mechanisation; and coupled with the steam engine, used in spinning since 1785, the history of capital and labour became one in which machinery steadily ousted handwork in one branch of industry after another.

Engels proceeds to elaborate this sketch, but the outlines are clear enough here for our purposes. What we have is a delineation of economic change which rests on the identification of technical innovation and its socio-economic consequences; the periodisation of the actual inventions provides the parameters of the history derived from this, and also identifies the principal problem: the conflict of labour and machinery, in which the introduction of the latter displaces the former. This was in fact the theme of the writings of the 1820s, expressed in Barton's

Observations on the Circumstances which Influence the Condition of the Labouring Classes of Society (1817), a text which was to lead to Ricardo revising the third edition of his *Principles* in which he abandoned the argument that labour displaced by machinery would simply find employment elsewhere. From the beginning then, as soon as the notion of industrialisation and its founding moment emerged, it was associated with the problem of labour and machinery. Whether an optimist like Ure, celebrating the new machine technology, or a pessimist like Barton, the emergence of the notion of 'Industrial Revolution' coincides with the consideration of the effects of mechanisation on labour.

Part of the reason for the late application of the term 'industrialisation' to denote these problems can be traced in the shifts in meaning that this required. Until the later eighteenth century, 'industry' was a characterisation of human activity. Ferguson for example in his *Essay on the History of Civil Society* uses the term in association with progress and civilisation; 'industry' is *learnt* by mankind as the necessary activity for the achievement of future reward, gradually forming the 'habits of the labourer, the mechanic, and the trader' (Ferguson, 1966, p. 97). The progress of society is dependent on the development of industry – but here 'industry' could be easily replaced by 'industriousness', unlike in the modern sense of the phrase. This can be seen in the following passage:

> The growth of industry, the endeavours of men to improve their arts, to extend their commerce, to secure their possessions, and to establish their rights, are indeed the most effectual means to promote population: but they arise from a different motive; they arise from regards to interest and personal safety. They are intended for the benefit of those who exist, not to procure the increase of their numbers.
>
> (Ferguson, 1966, p. 140)

The 'growth of industry' here does not denote the development of industrial production as a generic form of productive activity taking place under definite conditions; it is simply *synonymous with* that which follows it, the 'endeavours of men', useful and consciously directed labour on the part of mankind. It is the action of a subject, not a type of economic organisation.

Although the article entitled 'Industrie' in the *Encyclopédie* of 1765 employs a rather different definition, in which a particular kind of work is designated, there is a basic similarity with the usage of Ferguson:

> This word signifies two things: either simple manual labour or inventions of the mind producing useful machines, relating to arts and trades; *industry* includes sometimes the one, sometimes the other, and sometimes unites both.
>
> It relates to the culture of land, to manufactures and the arts. (cited in Lough, 1971, p. 359)

Here the term is associated more directly with the process of manufacturing, and the article does go on to consider the manufacturing enterprises of France. Nevertheless, the term still signifies the activity of a person, be it manual or mental, with respect to a defined class of objects, noted in the last sentence; and the fact that 'industry' refers indifferently to land, manufactures and 'arts' only serves to underline the absence of a distinction according to one particular form of economic activity or organisation.

This is also clear in the Introduction to the *Wealth of Nations*, where Smith refers to 'industry' in similar terms:

> The policy of some nations has given extraordinary encouragement to the industry of the country; that of others to the industry of towns. Scarce any nation has dealt equally and impartially with every sort of industry. Since the downfall of the Roman Empire, the policy of Europe has been more favourable to arts, manufactures, and commerce, the industry of towns; than to agriculture, the industry of the country. (Smith, 1976, p. 11)

Nothing could be clearer than this application of the term indifferently to commerce, manufacture and agriculture, and elsewhere in the book Smith makes the sense even more precise by setting 'industry' up in opposition to 'idleness' (p. 335). So when Smith considers the 'quantity of industry which any capital can employ' (p. 295) he is referring to the capacities of a labouring population, not to a sector of an economy.

Not until the 1830s did it become customary to talk of 'industry' and 'industrialism' as pertaining to sectors of an economy or types of social organisation, embodied in institutional forms. This did not displace the earlier usage entirely, but it does disappear from economic treatises; while Smith's concern was to promote the strength of a nation through the combination of sound policy with an industrious population, this exact configuration of nation, policy and population cannot be found in Ricardo, nor in the writings of the 1820s.

In fact consideration of the historical etymology of 'industry' and its associated linguistic modifications will not illuminate the formation of the concept of 'industrial revolution', or even the nature of 'industrial society'. The emergence of these conceptions is dependent on the transformation of a semantic field in which a more strategic part is played by the terminology referring to places of work and production – 'manufacture', 'mechanical arts', 'factory', 'workshop' and 'mill'. What will first emerge is the apparent quaintness, by modern linguistic standards, of the language used to describe the 'industrial revolution'; but then it should become clearer that more is at issue than styles of expression.

Consider this passage from Ferguson's *Essay*:

> Many mechanical arts, indeed, require no capacity; they succeed best under a total suppression of sentiment and reason; and ignorance is the mother of industry as well as of superstition. Reflection and fancy are subject to err; but a habit of moving the hand, or the foot, is independent of either. Manufactures, accordingly, prosper most, where the mind is least consulted, and where the workshop may, without any great effort of imagination, be considered as an engine, the parts of which are men.
>
> (Ferguson, 1966, pp. 182–3)

'Mechanical' here refers not to machines, but to repetitive actions on the part of labourers; and 'manufacture' is associated with the combination of mechanical labour into a workshop, in which the parts of the 'engine' are men, not machines. Marx drew attention to the distinction between such manufactories and factories in the modern sense, assigning the former to the period before industrialisation proper; and the *Encyclopédie* underlines this by distinguishing between centralised manufactories and dispersed manufactories, processes taking place under one roof in the case of the former, and in the home of the labourer in the case of the latter. Not only is this distinction drawn (the editor of the English summary quite wrongly referring to the first as 'factories'), but the writer of the article goes on to state the opinion that domestic industry has many advantages over centralised manufacturing (Lough, 1971, pp. 361–2).

In fact the French terms for 'factory' (*fabrique*, *usine*) do not permit the confusion between 'manufactory' and 'factory' as in English. In the early eighteenth century for example, *manufacture* designated a *place* and *fabrique* a form of action, while *usine* related only at this time to water-driven enterprises in northeast France (Baldinger, 1963, pp. 323, 331). In English, the dominant usage at this time for 'factory' derived from its association with 'agency', being employed for instance to denote establishments set up by traders operating in a foreign country. Technically, 'manufacture' during the earlier part of the eighteenth century referred to anything 'made by art', the productions of a place or country, or a site of production. Consequently, the line between 'manufactory' and 'factory' in the eighteenth century does not lie between handwork on the one hand and mechanical labour on the other, although Marx among others later used such a distinction (Freudenberger, Redlich, 1964, p. 386). During this period, the terms were in some sense interchangeable, and did not refer exclusively to forms of enterprise of distinct types; and while 'factory' was generally used to refer to sets of buildings, it can also be legitimately asked why this became the modern term for an industrial enterprise, rather than 'fabrick', which also had a similar currency in the earlier part of the century as a term for the buildings within which work was performed. This is after all the term which became customary in Germany (Hilger, 1975).

The 'factories' of the eighteenth century in which material was worked up by machinery under the supervision of labourers were on the other hand usually referred to as 'mills', that is, according to their source of power. Ure in his *Philosophy of Manufactures* published in 1835 defined a factory accordingly:

> The term *Factory*, in technology, designates the combined operation of many orders of work-people, adult and young, in tending with assiduous skill a system of productive machines continuously impelled by a central power. (p. 13)

This was distinguished by Ure from the simple concentration and co-operation of workers in breweries, carpenter's shops and similar occupations. Tann, in her survey of factory development, found this definition too restrictive (1970, p. 3), but it is important to note the manner in which Ure insists on such restriction. He is quite clear that what is to be excluded are manufactories, in fact all enterprises not based on machine technology and centralised power. This takes the problem of machinery and labour further than many contemporary writers, and locates the conflict as between labourers on the one hand, and the owners, not simply of a new technology, but of a new system of economic organisation and social domination. Ure, Babbage and others are the first theorists of a new social order, and in their works they proceed to delineate the mechanisms and relations of this order in a fashion which breaks with that of the past. It only remained for this new social order to be summarised in the phrase 'Industrial Revolution'.

The discrepancy between the phrase and the period which it signifies that appears in Engels' usage is therfore partially explained. Terms such as 'Industrial Revolution' and 'industrialisation' to denote the economic development of Britain in the later eighteenth century are formulated in a tardy fashion because the set of semantic relations on which they are based detaches itself only very slowly from a 'pre-industrial' vocabulary. Discussions of the economy in the late eighteenth century, subordinated as they are to this obsolete terminology, have great difficulty coming to terms with the changes going on at that time.

At least this would be one explanation, but it is not really very satisfactory. It represents a compromise: between a representational theory of language and the history books which say that the economy, which such language is conceived as representing, is changing rapidly from 1760 onwards. Indeed, we would be in even deeper trouble if the writings of history books were taken absolutely at their word, for it is not until the 1880s, with Toynbee's *Lectures on the Industrial Revolution of the 18th. Century in England* that a text emerges that takes as its object the set of events labelled the 'Industrial Revolution'. Clark in his examination of the 'idea of the Industrial Revolution' noted that historians often fail to agree on the nature and periodisation of this revolution, sometimes suggesting that a reconciliation of the discrepancies would be of little value. But the dislocations between the accounts provided in the history books and the manner in which economic analysis developed can be treated as symptoms of a problem: either of the relation of language to a reality as defined by the writing of history, or more simply, as a symptom of a breakdown in the writing of histories.

Exploration of this problem requires that more be said about the features of the Industrial Revolution presented to us by the historians. At the same time, it is necessary to remember that the provenance of the term is not limited to those texts which directly address themselves to it. The conception of an Industrial Revolution as a founding moment of modern English society is one that is fundamental to school textbooks, economic journalism and television documentaries; it is regarded as the paradigmatic case of industrialisation by economic historians and television producers alike. Despite its late start, the term has long since entered the public domain, and any historian writing on the subject must necessarily take this into account.

How then did Toynbee set about identifying the Industrial Revolution in the first set of lectures on the subject?

> The Essence of the Industrial Revolution is the substitution of competition for the medieval regulations which had previously controlled the production and distribution of wealth. (Toynbee, 1890, p. 85)

This of course cannot serve as an account of the actual structure of the Industrial Revolution, for all it states is that competition instead of monopoly and control characterises the progress of the economy. Relying rather too heavily on the *Wealth of Nations*, Toynbee does, despite the error of such a declaration, depart interestingly from the customary listing of factors in industrial growth; and while he later proceeds to enumerate such a list, this implicit reference to *capitalism* rather than *industrialism* as the essence of the Industrial Revolution is highly significant. Few historians following Toynbee could be said to have opened up such a possibility.

Four main features characterise the industrial revolution, according to Toynbee:

(1) the rapid growth of population;
(2) the decline of an agricultural population, associated with

the agrarian revolution which had enclosed fields and consolidated farms;

(3) the substitution of the factory for the domestic system – embodied in the spinning jenny, Arkwright's water frame, Crompton's mule, and the self-acting mule of 1792, which was not however used until 1825;

(4) the improvement of communications, especially the canal system. (Toynbee, 1890, pp. 87–91)

The list is remarkably similar to the one presented by Engels, and is one which, in effect, constantly constitutes the major features of the industrial revolution in historical writings up to the present day. What is significant in such a set of factors is that 'industrialism' is grasped primarily as a system of techniques, albeit techniques with definite social effects. The chronology of the revolution revolves around the dates of invention or introduction of these techniques, and, tacitly, around tha cotton industry. In fact it is not even the whole cotton industry for the eighteenth century, but rather that section concerned with the preparation and spinning of yarn. Until the introduction of the power loom, the rapid growth in spinning was met by a steady augmentation of handloom weaving. The 'cotton industry', even more so the 'textile industry', was characterised until quite late by a combination of mechanised and handwork processes which were mutually interdependent. Even though it was the leading element in the revolution, according to conventional accounts, it would be wrong to associate even cotton as a whole with factory production.

This is however the image that comes over in many accounts of the period, in which the Industrial Revolution is pictured as an age, dating from the later eighteenth century, of factories and steam power, of fat capitalists and impoverished wage workers, of machinery, discipline and regulation. Such images are on an epic scale: the accumulation of capital, the creation of new machinery, the advance of steam as a power source completely altering the spatial structure of the economy, the dragooning of a reluctant labour force into factory routines and rhythms of work, the development of industrial slums of an ever-increasing scale. All dominated by cotton, imported from the slave plantations of the United States, worked up into cloth in the new factories, the foundation of British exports in an economy whose development was to depend crucially on the export of finished goods.

Like any epic however, such an image feeds on a desire for great moments of history to emerge in a garb fitting to the occasion. And while it cannot be denied that certain very significant things began to happen in the later eighteenth century in the British economy, the beginnings of industrial capitalism were very patchy and spasmodic, hardly rating a supporting travelogue let alone a Panavision epic. The combination of important shifts in balance and a few critical changes within an economy which proceeded onward according to a predominantly agricultural cycle creates problems for the historian seeking to write the history of the Industrial Revolution, especially since most of the witnesses who can be rounded up seem to have been blind to its reality. And so a certain tension arises in the writing of this history, in which the demands of common knowledge conflict with the evidence that can be assembled.

We can take Hobsbawm's *Industry and Empire* as an example – appropriate perhaps not least on account of its appearance in paperback in 1969 as part of the Pelican Economic History of Britain, and thus a widely read text. Dating the Industrial Revolution between 1780 and 1840, the third chapter of this book begins with the statement 'Whoever says Industrial Revolution says cotton' (p. 56). While this slogan does not exhaust the features of the revolution,

> cotton was the pacemaker of industrial change, and the basis of the first regions which could not have existed but for industrialisation, and which expressed a new form of society, industrial capitalism, based on a new form of production, the 'factory'. (p. 56)

In this way Hobsbawm places the general analysis of the Industrial Revolution firmly within the framework of the epic that his reading public have come to expect – it is a book designed for a popular readership, and must needs begin from the conception of a popular historiography. Accordingly many of the elements of analysis that can be found in Engels and Toynbee are presented, such as factories, workers, capitalists, and foremost of all, machinery which is the measure and form of technical progress. It might appear then that this history of the Industrial

Revolution is simply destined to repeat, with some variations, the technicist history of the industrialisation of the British economy, in which machines ineluctably alter the lives of the individuals who make up the social order.

There is however in *Industry and Empire* a subsidiary narrative which continually subverts the epic narrative. Consider the following passage:

> The early Industrial Revolution was technically rather primitive not because no better science and technology was available, or because men took no interest in it or could not be persuaded to use it. It was simple because, by and large, the application of simple ideas and devices, often of ideas available for centuries, often by no means expensive, could produce striking results. (Hobsbawm, 1969, p. 60)

Therefore the revolutionary nature of the later eighteenth century is traced not to massive accumulations of capital, nor to the sudden invention of technologies that superseded all others, but rather to a reorganisation and implementation of what was available in new ways. And this is why the epic nature of the Industrial Revolution becomes a problem: the tangible signs of progress are hard to find, and consequently what visible changes there are taking place are seized upon as constitutive of the revolution itself.

Hobsbawm sets out in a conventional manner from these visible changes, but increasingly qualifies the history which runs naturally from them. He emphasises for example that coal and iron consumption was sporadic until the development of the railways, and that extensive sectors of productive activity in the economy carried on in the traditional ways, meeting increasing demand for their products through an intensification of the domestic system. 'Factory production' was not a possibility for furniture, clothing, building and many engineering trades – and while their products were increasingly required by an expanding domestic and foreign market, mechanisation or even centralisation was not a feasible option for the organisation of production (Hobsbawm, 1969, p. 71). Until the 1830s and 1840s states Hobsbawm, drawing on calculations made by Phyllis Deane, gross capital formation never exceeded 10 per cent per annum. The apparently low levels of investment of the period

1760–1830, according to later standards of industrialisation, are in fact even lower than Hobsbawm suggests, since early investment was not only low, it was mostly taken up with repair and maintenance of existing stocks of fixed capital, as Higgins and Pollard have emphasised (1971). During the early period of the 'Industrial Revolution' investment was more in circulating than fixed capital, just like the typical pattern of investment in manufactories as opposed to factories.

A second phase of industrialisation is identified by Hobsbawm in the years 1840–95, based initially around railway construction, ushering in the rise of the iron and coal industries, and displacing the crisis-ridden cotton industry as the leading element of British industrial growth:

> With the railways Britain therefore entered the period of full industrialisation. Its economy was no longer dangerously poised on the narrow platform of two or three pioneer sectors – notably textiles – but broadly based on a foundation of capital goods production, which in turn facilitated the advance of modern technology and organisation – or what passed for modern in the mid-nineteenth century – into a wide variety of industries. (Hobsbawm, 1969, p. 119)

The railways, significant not for their contribution to communications so much as for the manner in which their heavy use of steel virtually created a steel industry, are a more appropriate and adequate sign of industrialisation than the features of the eighteenth century, in which the image of factory and machine sits uneasily. Perhaps it could be suggested that the early sections of *Industry and Empire* contain two opposed themes: one of the conventional periodisation and identification of the Industrial Revolution, and one of a 'second phase' which consists of the kind of large-scale changes that are usually projected back to the later eighteenth century.

Provisionally, and with some reservations, this makes possible a solution to the problem with which this essay opened. The answer to the question: why did no one talk of an Industrial Revolution until the 1830s is – because it was not until that time that anything very considerable happened to the economy. Or, in other words, if we are to retain the terminology of the Industrial Revolution, it must be employed to refer not to the late eighteenth century, but rather to the third and fourth decades of the nineteenth, whose features are commonly projected back on to events occurring between sixty and eighty years previously.

Such a move can be justified simply by reference to modern accounts of the organisation of the late-eighteenth-century economy. The most recent and authoritative account of steam power in the period up to 1860 suggests that if all steam power sources had been replaced by alternatives like wind and water, the accumulated setback to the national income in 1800 would have amounted to two months at the most (von Tunzelman, 1978, p. 287). Steam, the symbol of the new age, was in fact dwarfed at this time by more mundane power sources. Arkwright's first purpose-built mill was constructed at Nottingham in 1769 to be powered by horses; and this was followed in 1771 by a water-powered establishment (Tann, 1970, p. 7). In some cases new 'factories' were founded simply by the conversion of old corn mills to new purposes.

It has also been suggested that the size of new mills and factories was determined not by factors such as the type of power source or transport costs, but rather according to the capital available over a long-term period. The length of time needed to construct and bring into operation the machinery of such enterprises led in many cases to the leasing of parts of completed buildings on the grounds that not until a few years had passed could they be filled with equipment (Tann, 1970, pp. 27-31). This machinery in turn, the 'famous inventions' listed above, were for the most part developed for the application of human, animal or water-power, and the importance of the first in even the 'progressive' cotton industry is not to be underestimated (von Tunzelman, 1978, p. 295). As Pollard has emphasised in his *Genesis of Modern Management*, the techniques did not exist until the mid-nineteenth century for supervising large bodies of labour in such a way that their concentration brought benefits of 'scale'; until this happened, size meant chaos.

These points, and they could be extended without any problem at all, serve however merely to assert that the customary manner of dealing with the Industrial Revolution is erroneous: the epic image that this series of events is granted is one that is unjustified. Two different conclusions could be drawn from this – either the 'Revolution' as such never took place in the eighteenth century, but later; or there were changes, but not the tangible and symbolic ones upon which so many accounts draw. If the first option is taken, one is too easily led into a revision which simply displaces a privileged set of techniques and objects and replaces them with yet another at a different place and time. The second is more appropriate to the argument here, for it both accounts for the lapses and paradoxes outlined above, and places in question the function of terms such as the 'Industrial Revolution' in the identification of periods of change in economic organisation.

It can be suggested that what begins to happen in the later eighteenth century is a reorganisation of production, distribution and consumption, in which alterations in the first of these become increasingly influenced by calculations concerning the nature of the second and third. To focus on the production process alone, and treating it as a site upon which labour meets machinery, is an error. This leads only to the kind of 'symbolic technicism' criticised earlier, in which change must needs be dramatic and sudden. Revolutionary change in economic organisation does not lie here; it can be traced instead to alterations in the disposal and arrangement of available resources. Indicators of such changes on anything other than enterprise-by-enterprise level are hard to come by, and make generalisation difficult.

One instance can perhaps be isolated by way of illustration. It might appear that the kind of analysis that is being proposed is one that would simply treat reorganisations of production and distribution in terms of a model of increasing rationality, more efficient means being employed to achieve the established ends of profit-making. Such a model might be associated with the history of capitalism to be found in the writings of Weber and Sombart. In this fashion, it would be possible to cite the activity of Josiah Wedgwood as the exemplar of profit-through-rationalism, and McKendrick has sought to show, contrary to Pollard, the importance of management controls and calculation among eighteenth-century entrepreneurs. While noting that the problem of costs in relation to profit only became of interest to Wedgwood in times of trade depression, he outlines the elaborate costing procedures used to establish the cost of a range of products in the Wedgwood pottery in 1772. These are indeed very detailed, and do appear to provide the information which would be needed for the appropriate calculation of prices and costs. Cost accounting emerges here, according to McKendrick, as a rational instrument of industrial organisation (1970, pp. 48, 50–1). But there are major problems in this schema; for one thing, Wedgwood forgot his own wages and the costs of experiment and research, seriously underestimating his own costs (Thomas, 1971, p. 129). Second, the costs arrived at with such elaborate calculation were not used in the determination of wages nor of wholesale or retail prices. The wages of even skilled workers were determined primarily by their availability, while prices were 'fancy', varying according to Wedgwood's estimation of a customer's ability to pay. The calculation of wage levels on the one hand, and the price structure of finished goods on the other, was unrelated to cost of production; and in any case such wide margins existed that there was rarely any need to assess costs and revenue in an elaborate fashion. Far from being an instrument of rationalism, Wedgwood's cost accounting was of the same order as Louis XVI's lock-repairing activities: a technical hobby. The profitability of the Wedgwood concern was based not on progressive entrepreneurial techniques as such, but rather on the ability to mass-produce objects of fashionable consumption; and when trade was particularly brisk, Wedgwood was not above buying up the imitations of his competitors to sell under his own mark. This signifies sound business judgement it is true, but there is nothing which distinguishes this as a peculiarly capitalistic device.

While however the alterations in consumption and distribution of goods might have been neglected in treatments of the 'Industrial Revolution' which focussed naturally on the production sphere, this essay can do no more than indicate some of the limitations of such a concern. The suggestion that the 'Industrial Revolution' and its associated terminology is best forgotten is impelled by a number of motives, some of which have been outlined above. But there is an additional consideration which renders a sometimes arcane discussion of historical semantics of more immediate relevance: the fact that popular discussion of the effects of silicon chips on social and economic organisation in the 1980s replicates many of the issues raised above. The use of the phrase 'second Industrial Revolution' to describe the potentially progressive yet disruptive effects of chip technology retraces exactly the contours of arguments among which the term 'Industrial Revolution' was first coined to describe and summarise recent technological changes. Even a brief survey of the literature of the 1820s and 1830s shows that two opposed positions rapidly crystallised, each of which presupposed a fetishisation of machine technology: one school of thought maintaining that all those displaced from jobs by machinery would find employment elsewhere; and the other maintaining that the net effect would be structural unemployment.

After Ricardo had gone over from the first school to the second with the publication of the third edition of *Principles* in 1821, the principal representative of the first school in the 1820s was McCulloch, whose thought on the subject is well-summarised in the following bland statement:

> It appears, therefore, that no improvement of machinery can possibly diminish the demand for labour, or reduce the rate of wages. The introduction of machinery into one employment, *necessarily occasions an equal or greater demand for the disengaged labourers in some other employment.* The only hardship which it ever imposes on the labourer, is, that in some cases it forces him to change his business.
>
> (McCulloch, 1821, p. 115)

In some general sense this statement is true enough, but it presupposes that social and economic conditions exist which permit the foundation of new enterprises and the relocation of labour. It was on the other hand not the most propitious time for an economist to appeal to market forces; the growing plight of the weavers in this period was a ready example of the suffering caused when the worker was 'forced to change his business'.

The argument which proposed that the result of machine industry was bound to be structural unemployment was expounded by Barton in the first few pages of his pamphlet *Observations on the Circumstances which Influence the Condition of the Labouring Classes of Society*, taking exception to the thesis according to which the demand for labour was strictly related to the rise of national wealth. First introducing some historical examples from the British economy that demonstrated recurrent problems of unemployment and destitution, this is then demonstrated with 'sound reasoning'.

> It does seem that every accession of capital necessarily sets in motion an additional quantity of labour. Let us suppose a

> case. – A manufacturer possesses a capital of 1,000 l. which he employs in maintaining twenty weavers, paying them 50 l. per annum each. His capital is suddenly increased to 2,000 l. By double means he does [not] however hire double the number of workmen, but lays out 1,500 l. in erecting machinery, by the help of which five men are enabled to perform the same quantity of work as twenty did before. Are not then fifteen men discharged in consequence of the manufacturer having increased his capital? (Barton, 1817, p. 15)

Subsequent adjustments moderate this to a net loss of ten jobs, three workers being employed constantly in the manufacture and repair of machinery, while the manufacturer himself employs two domestic servants with his increased income.

This numerical reasoning is then supported by the division of capital into fixed and circulating parts, only the latter being used for the support of labour. The extension of the economy however results in the former growing at a faster rate than the latter, and only if these two parts of capital increase in proportion with each other can structural unemployment be avoided. Destitution and poverty then are for Barton the necessary correlates of mechanisation.

There are of course a number of weaknesses in this argument and its form of presentation. The numerical example is for instance entirely hypothetical, it would be possible to construct a model which demonstrated the opposite result. Similarly, the effect of technological change is only assessed with respect to the single enterprise, and the outcome generalised to the economy as a whole. The use of the distinction between fixed and circulating capital appears more plausible, but here again the conclusion rests on a speculated faster rate of fixed capital formation. Ricardo, while impressed by these arguments, did not simply take them over, and so his adoption of Barton's side did not involve him in committing similar errors. What is interesting about the new chapter on machinery however is that the 'problem' was derived through the consideration of the capital employed by a farmer/manufacturer and the year on year effects on his labour force. Thus again the displacement of labour was confined to short-term effects within one enterprise, and there was in fact no means of moving beyond this to the economy as a whole without leaving the terrain of economic theory and engaging in discussions of policies such as the Poor Laws.

In any case, both sides of the argument confined themselves to a consideration of the effects of machinery on labour as a simple polar opposition, which led to the new relations of power of a capitalist order, in part exercised through machine systems, being exclusively associated with the displacement of labour by machinery. The new technologies which were the subject of debate were however simply a physical manifestation of much deeper problems of supervision, authority and domination in a changing political order. It was not immediately obvious to the radicals of the early nineteenth century, nor the the revolutionaries who succeeded them, quite how these new systems of rule could be effectively challenged in a manner that achieved anything more than temporary immobilisation of one or more of the media through which domination was effected. Socialism as a political movement came to identify the factory of the capitalist as the crucial site of domination, with machinery and the organisation of work as its principal means. But such an identification is very partial, and has in fact hindered the effective development of a socialist politics capable of confronting questions of power outside a narrowly-defined economic terrain. It is therefore to be regretted that one hundred and fifty years after the problems of capitalist society were identified with the effects of machine technologies, the debates on the consequences of the 'Second Industrial Revolution' can do little more than recapitulate the terms of an earlier debate.

4 The 'Histories' of Economic Discourse*

It is commonplace today to find Adam Smith and 'his book' – *An Inquiry into the Nature and Causes of the Wealth of Nations* – treated as founding modern economics, both in the pronouncements of ideologists of the market economy and in the judgements of historians of economics. That in some way the work of Smith is a turning point in the 'history of economics' is clear from those accounts which address themselves to the forerunners of 'modern economics' (Gordon, 1975; Johnson, 1937; Taylor, 1965), where Smith is taken as the end-point of such prehistories. The placing of Smith as the origin of modernism, while providing convenient timetables for the arrangement of histories, does however raise some fundamental historiographical questions concerning the object of a history of economics, and the manner in which it is organised. Such questions (which form the problems considered in the first section of this essay) are usually speedily dismissed in orthodox histories by the invocation of a set of devices which constitute their methodological stock-in-trade: the identification of neglected predecessors, the construction of terminological biographies, the identification of a 'philosophical heritage', the discussion of theoretical influence, and so on. Two major difficulties can be said to emerge in such writing: firstly, what is the alleged 'history of economics' a history of? (what is the object of this discourse?); and secondly, what is *historical* about this 'history'?

There are of course solutions already given to these apparently 'unnecessary' questions, albeit sometimes manifested in a rather vulgar fashion. The solutions are, respectively: the history of economics traces the emergence of a systematic analysis of the

*First published in *Economy and Society* Vol. 6 (1977)

economy; and in so doing, places the writings it designates in their context. These seemingly simple formulations do nevertheless conceal a series of problems, which will be briefly enumerated below. The relevance of such an exposition will then be shown by considering the structure of perhaps the most systematic treatment of Smith's 'economics' that has so far appeared, that presented by Hollander in his avowedly neo-classical *Economics of Adam Smith*. But the major purpose of this essay is not to produce another critique of secondary texts, and accordingly the argument will then move on to consider the significance of the new edition of Smith's works (in fact, the first complete edition). Finally it will be suggested that the significance of *The Wealth of Nations* can be traced not to the 'timeliness' of Smith's inspiration, but rather to the function of the text in the theoretical debates of the early nineteenth century.

The 'economic' nature of the *Wealth of Nations* is not given, expressed in the instant of its writing for all time; specific discursive conditions are required for it to be read as a work of economic *theory*, rather that (as in the late eighteenth century) a work of *legislation*, and these discursive conditions arise quite suddenly in the early nineteenth century. Dugald Stewart, in his authoritative assessment of *The Wealth of Nations,* clearly places the work as a contribution to the understanding of legislative action on the part of states:

> To direct the policy of nations with respect to one most important class of its laws, those which form its system of political economy, is the great aim of Mr. Smith's *Inquiry*: and he has unquestionably had the merit of presenting to the world, the most comprehensive and perfect work that has yet appeared, on the general principles of any branch of legislation. The example which he has set will be followed, it is to be hoped, in due time, by other writers, for whom the internal policy of states furnishes many other subjects of discussion no less curious and interesting . . .
>
> (Stewart, 1811, pp. 81-2)

This conception of the primary import of the work as in a branch of legislation rather than establishing a new discourse of economic theory was also shared by Buchanan in his *Observations on the Subjects treated of in Dr. Smith's Inquiry into the Nature and Causes of the Wealth of Nations* (1814, p. viii); although Buchanan believed Smith continually converted issues of *policy* into issues of *economy*. But by economy here Buchanan means *cheapness*, not a new conception of the economic order (Buchanan, 1814, pp. x–xi).

As will be shown, it is the critique of Smith conducted by Ricardo that is instrumental in converting *The Wealth of Nations* into the classical foundation of economic theory, intitating a particular reading of the text that has survived to the present.

This radical disjunction of the *writing* and the *readings* of a text, a disjunction which is obliterated in the practice of the history of ideas, must in no way be confused with the classical conception of the interpretation of a text, since such a notion carries with it the assumption of a privileged original meaning inscribed by a particular *subject* at a particular *time*. The history of ideas concerns itself with the discovery of this original meaning in a search for the author and his inspirations (biography) and the assignation of these to a particular temporal location (date). The interpenetration of biographies and dates thence constitutes the fabric of such historical writings. The proposition that Smith (the man representing his text) is the originator of modern economics is thereby rendered as the work of an inspired authorial subject who goes beyond the texts of earlier authorial subjects.

This characterisation of the enterprise of a history of ideas is naturally a very general one and has to be elaborated further. In the case of history of economics, the problem remains to be answered: which are the texts and writers that are to be canvassed? The archive of writing that is to be searched must in some way be delimited, it must be possible in some fashion to identify those writings that are central to any projected history. Manifestly there are here some major problems to be dealt with even if the basic definition is assumed to be 'writing which addresses itself to the study of the economy'. As the histories of mercantilism show, unless there is some means of distinguishing legislation on the administration of a national economy from 'economic theory', the history of economic analysis becomes confused with a chronology of economic edicts. Again, the history of economics provides itself with a device that permits it to demarcate the domain of its historical investigation. This device is the operation of a simple teleology, or as Bachelard formulates it, the *recurrent* reworking of the history of a science as the history of its progress. This produces a double history, in the form of a *sanctioned* history of the positive acts producing the knowledge, and a continually augmented *peripheral* history made up from the discarded elements in the progress of the science (Bachelard, 1965, pp. 24–7). Perhaps the most well-known example of such an exercise is Schumpeter's *History of Economic Analysis*, which, beginning with the Greeks, divides up the progress of economic thought into a series of 'advances' and 'errors', in which the 'advances' are in the surreptitious formulation of the principles of Walrasian general equilibrium analysis. The procedure for Aristotle, for example, is to ascribe the 'clarifications' of value, price and capital in his writings to 'far-sightedness', while attributing the lapses with respect to modern theory to contemporary circumstances (Schumpeter, 1954a, pp. 59–65; 1954b, pp. 11–13).

The history of economics then is constituted by the genesis of modern economic theory, and this genesis is realised through the superimposition of the structure of neo-classical economics on the monuments of this history. This procedure takes care of the *object* of the history of economics, but still leaves unexplained the timetable of this history. If this is to be accounted for as anything more than the differential analysis of writings, the obvious solution is to examine the form of development of the relevant 'context'. Economic theory is the theory of the economy: the chronology of theory must therefore in some way be related to the chronology of the economy. Stated in this fashion, the proposition seems innocuous; but once developed into a particular narrative, substantial problems appear. In the case of Smith, the form this takes is to argue that his economics is formed by the contemporary economy, and, writing as he does at the threshold of capitalism, *The Wealth of Nations* is moulded by the material which it works. *The Wealth of Nations* is the embodiment of nascent capitalism. Roll in his classical study for example argues that mercantile capital 'produces' mercantilism, and industrial capital 'produces' political economy, such that Classical Political Economy is explained as the abstract reflection of industrial production (Roll, 1954, pp. 93ff.). It is difficult to envisage such an approach being effective in any serious consideration of specific writings, and it is not surprising that having established such a general framework, the actual history is constituted by Roll as a succession of authors.

A reduction of theoretical discourse to the circumstances in which it appears to be uttered, the substitution of economic history for history of economics, is necessarily mediated by an experiencing subject. The form this argument takes with writings on Smith, as we shall see below, is first to argue that certain forms of production existed; second to determine whether such forms are dealt with in the text; and third to ascertain whether Smith in fact knew of their existence. The first two items can of course be settled in a relatively straightforward fashion, while the third leaves open a range of possibilities for investigation and conjecture, possibilities which are extensively explored in the literature of the history of economics. The effectivity of 'real history' on theory can only be formulated as the experience of an authorial subject, a subject who is constitutive of the text by virtue of the privileged conjuncture that he occupies as the mediator of experience and a written heritage. To place this subject in history, with his thoughts and experiences, is to write the history of economics.

If this privilege, granting the author and his text an original meaning fixed in experience once and for all, is rejected, the whole basis of a history of ideas begins to collapse. A series of questions can then be asked:

(1) in precisely what form does 'the economy' irrupt into economic discourse?

(2) what is the basis on which we can demarcate an economic discourse while (a) eschewing the use of modern theory to direct us to such discourses and (b) rejecting the conventional chronological periodisation of the history of ideas?[1]

(3) why should we accept that the writer of a text is a principle of its unity?

This essay of course merely aims to pose such questions by means of a discussion of Adam Smith and his 'economic writing', rather than pretend to an adequate assessment of such problems. Stated as bald answers to such questions, however, the following can be said. Firstly, the problem concerning the relation of the world of concrete real objects to the world of thought presupposes that thought is distinct from the real. It can be argued however that discourse is material, and that there is no way in which a supposed 'more real' economy can be used to assess the effectivity of a discursive order. There is no longer the 'ideal' and the 'material': there is instead the discursive and the non-discursive.[2] The problem of the relevance of economic thought to its 'time' is thereby effaced, and attention directed to the theoretical and material conditions of existence of an economic discourse.

Secondly, the criteria of what constitutes an 'economic discourse' can in no way be dealt with via the imposition of a neo-classical (or, in another variation, a Marxist) grid, organising the rational and the irrational of the archive according to the dictates of a privileged theoretical structure, tracing its precursors in its own reflection. In fact, it might be suggested that a thorough knowledge of contemporary economic theory is a great handicap to any prospective historian, since the illusion is thereby fostered in the practical work of investigation that in some way at least the nature of economic discourse is unproblematic (although such a remark is engendered more by reflection on the nature of contemporary economic theory). The detailed examination of the conditions of formation of particular discourses is a task quite distinct from the theoretical development of these discourses, and requires an apparatus appropriate to such a project. While such an apparatus cannot be specified in advance, it can be said that treatment of modern theory as the source of concepts and forms of explanation universally characteristic of economic discourse is bound to produce teleological and erroneous accounts.

Finally, what has gone before indicates that to cast the writer as constitutive author is simply a phase in a process of reduction which follows from the empiricist distinction of the thought and the real. Particular texts are not the creation of an inspired author, but are the product of specific discursive and non-discursive conditions. But the conditions in which any such text is read and re-read transform that text, there is no inherent stability of such writing. This essay will later begin to show quite how this works.

In many ways Hollander's *Economics of Adam Smith* is one of the more systematic treatments of *The Wealth of Nations*: indeed, the comments on the back cover attributed to Lord Robbins which describes the book as 'one of the most distinguished essays in the history of economic thought of the last quarter of a century' indicate that we are dealing here with a text that is rated highly by eminent historians. To describe it in such a fashion however provides no idea of the nature of the argument – for while being a 'systematic treatment' of Smith's economics, it must be asked what *kind* of treatment it is. Two general remarks can be made at once concerning this text:

(1) in dealing with *The Wealth of Nations* there is not an even distribution of attention through the text; it is the first two books (out of five) that are concentrated on;
(2) the form of organisation of the text and the chapters relies on the pre-given coherence of neo-classical theory, with particular emphasis given to the theory of price and equilibrium analysis.

Blaug pointed out some years ago in his *Economic Theory in Retrospect* (a title that speaks volumes) that the version of Smith familiar to economists derived from a truncated *Wealth of Nations*, where the first two books are assimilated to modern theory, and the bulk of the work, dealing with problems of population, administration, and a critical treatment of a set of predecessors, is virtually ignored (Blaug, 1968). As will be shown below, there are serious difficulties that arise in an approach which divides the book into the 'relevant' and the 'irrelevant' for a history of economics.

For of course, and this brings us to the second point, the criterion of relevancy is derived from the structure of neo-classical theory. This practice of writing a history of Smith's economics creates Smith as the founder of modern economics in Books One and Two of *The Wealth of Nations*; a mirror is thereby created in which it can trace its own origins. These origins are, however, to be found not in the text composed in 1776, but rather in the reflection which such a history has itself constituted.

Hollander recognises that this is a problem, and he in fact begins in a roundabout fashion by discussing an article written by F. H. Knight in 1935, in which Ricardo is criticised for not formulating a neo-classical theory of price and distribution. Such rampant recurrence is rejected, and a more moderate form adopted:

> . . . we adopt the position that the use of modern analytical tools, concepts, and procedures may be of considerable aid

> in the analysis of the work of an early writer, *provided that he was operating within the general frame of reference for which these devices are appropriate*. In particular, we believe that there is justification for the utilisation of the current state of knowledge regarding the general equilibrium process in a study of the economics of Adam Smith insofar as he adopted the position that the price mechanism can be relied upon to clear product and factor markets. We therefore seek for the variety of equilibriating mechanisms which he assumed to bring about the result, utilising in the process the categories of modern theory. (Hollander, 1973, pp. 13-14.)

Thus the use of modern categories is predicated on the congruence of such categories with those in the text at issue. But Hollander introduces no criteria by which it would be possible to assess the basis of any possible congruency; and he is left with neo-classical theory as the only systematic mode for the analysis of the 'economic archive'. By default, therefore, his reconstruction of Smith's economics must result in the appearance of *The Wealth of Nations* as the origin of neo-classicism.

It must be stated that some attempt is made to go outside the body of contemporary economic theory for alternative approaches to the work of Smith, but, as is so often the case in contemporary history of economics, it is Kuhn's *Structure of Scientific Revolutions* which is turned to.[3] The introduction of terms such as 'paradigm' and 'normal science' (Hollander, 1973, p. 12) serve as metaphorical devices which enable the formulation of notions of 'structure' and 'change' in the development of a knowledge, without being able to deal with the process of the formation of this knowledge; nor does Kuhn deliver the analytical means with which to move away from this metaphor of revolution and study the functioning of constituted knowledges. It can be seem from the manner in which the ideas of Kuhn are introduced into the preliminary discussion of recurrence in the history of economics that the effect is to simply *relativise* the privileged theoretical apparatus (neo-classicism). The 'absolutism' of Knight is rejected by Hollander on the grounds that the theories of price and distribution which he deploys are simply part of a paradigm which one day may be replaced. The privilege of neo-classicism is thus removed *via* a gesture to a speculative theoretical future in which 'other theories' might emerge. Kuhn is employed to lend this future some substance with his box of tricks, but like all illusionists Kuhn relies on sleight of hand to provide the appearance of substance. Hollander is thus able to agnostically state that in the future things might be different, while maintaining that in the here and now neo-classical theory seems to be making progress, and that it is therefore the only suitable point of departure for a history of economic thought.

The dominance of recurrence as a methodological device in Hollander's account can be judged from the form of the first two major chapters, which set out to deal with the 'pre-Smithian' economic writings. The primacy of Smith is here assumed, and a series of texts are brought to the bar and criticised for the absences in their formulations. For instance, the following passage is simply one of many similar in these opening chapters:

> The published version of Hutcheson's lectures contains a chapter dealing with price, but the subject is carried no further than it had been by Pufendorf. It is clear that the fundamental hiatus in the analysis of price determination by the scholastic writers and the ethical jurists remained to be filled.
>
> (Hollander, 1973, p. 33)

This teleology unwinds itself through the major figures of 'eighteenth-century economics', endlessly establishing that in their position as forerunners of Smith, they could not write what Smith writes, and that as a consequence there were a series of deficiencies in this body of thought. But the 'body' as well as the 'absences' is constituted by the work of Smith, since they are doomed to chronologically come before the end to which they all merely contribute.

When Hollander turns in Chapter 3 to a consideration of Smith himself, he begins not with *The Wealth of Nations* but with the economic environment of Smith. In particular he is concerned to emphasise the industrial nature of production in the late eighteenth century, and he does this by considering the relative preponderance of agriculture and manufacturing. As he points out, it has become common in writing on Smith's economic milieu to stress the pre-industrial nature of the Scottish economy, writers arguing both that industrial technology was poorly developed at the time, and that even those processes which were developing seemed to have been ignored by Smith on the evidence presented in his economic writings (Hollander, 1973, p. 95, fn. 1). Such a form of argument is clearly based on the assumption that the 'economy' can be directly effective within writing on the economy, *via* the experience of an authorial subject. Argument therefore can take place concerning the level of development of the economy (particularly of the cotton industry, which later came to be identified as the critical sector of the developing industrial capitalist economy), and on whether the experience of Smith was an adequate reflection of this form of development.[4] Hollander adopts the view that Smith both knew of industrial advances (particularly the large-scale iron works at Carron) and incorporated the conclusions that he drew from such experience in his book. He concludes:

> As we shall see, Smith entered into a highly sophisticated analysis of the effect of scale of *industry* upon the degree of division of labour practised at the plant.
>
> (Hollander, 1973, p. 105)

Smith's treatment of the division of labour is therefore taken by Hollander to be an analysis of the organisation of the capitalist factory, and its adequacy is judged by the degree of its correspondence with 'real factories'. It will be shown below when dealing with *The Wealth of Nations* that if the division of labour is treated as a *concept*, rather than as a description of the disposition of labour in a building, conclusions can be drawn of a completely different order to those of Hollander.

This essay does not set out to provide an appreciation of the merits and demerits of various expositions of Smith taking as given the validity of the historiography deployed. The object is rather to question repeatedly the conclusions drawn in a body of writing on the basis of the forms of explanation and judgement that they set to work. The remarks on the text of Hollander above do not pretend to indicate the value of the book to those who wish to 'read about' Smith; they confine themselves to noting the inherent limitations and defects of a text which, as stated earlier, is good of its kind. It should also not be assumed that Hollander represents in his text the complete repertoire of the history of economics, as comparison with Napoleoni's account of Smith can serve to show.

Napoleoni's *Smith Ricardo Marx* presents an essay on each of these writers and in addition a chapter on the Physiocrats. Included with these essays is a collection of writings by the authors considered, in the case of Smith reprinting extracts from Cannan's edition of his *Lectures on Justice, Police, Revenue and Arms*. The overall intent of Napoleoni is to show that the changing nature of society has led to intellectual changes, and that in particular the rise of capitalism generated a reformulation of economic thought, in particular the treatment of the nature of value. The dangers inherent in such an exercise emerge relatively soon, for the Physiocrats are introduced only to be denounced for not having a theory of value (Napoleoni, 1975, p. 12).

The treatment of Smith however does differ from that of Hollander. Discussion does not take as its point of departure the structure of economic theory at present, but rather begins by locating the trends in moral philosophy in the mid-eighteenth century, and the manner in which Smith contributed to this body of thought in *The Theory of Moral Sentiments*. In this way it is possible to treat the *Wealth of Nations* as a text which is related to a body of thought which is non-economic, but which forms one of the principal theoretical conditions of existence for the 'economics' of Smith. Furthermore, by starting in this fashion it is possible to pose the problem of the forms taken by the *Wealth of Nations* in its progress from lectures on moral philosophy to an economic treatise. For example, the following judgement would not be found in the approach that Hollander takes, yet is intricately related to an understanding of Smith's 'economics':

> The *Lectures* specify that this process whereby wealth is increased through the spread of exchange has its roots in man's natural *rationality*; or rather that man, in so far as he is endowed with reason communicable through speech, can fully realise his nature only if he allows all his activities to be governed by the rule of communication and exchange.
>
> (Napoleoni, 1975, p. 34)

The basis established in this form of argument enables the various revisions of lectures and drafts of Smith's work to be better understood than in the unitary grid-reading that Hollander operates. Unfortunately after a promising start the dictates of the history of ideas reassert their grip, and the account of Smith rapidly slides into a version of the conventional Smithiana (the Glaswegian world in the late eighteenth century, the meeting with Turgot) that constitutes the parameters of the analysis of *Wealth of Nations* in modern writing. The position of Smith 'at the threshold' is finally described as follows:

> The real significance of this great thinker lies in his formulation, through a unique structure of thought, of nearly all the problems that were later taken up by further scientific thought, and especially important is his striking and nearly complete comprehension of the special nature of the new economic order that came into existence with the emergence of the bourgeoisie. (Napoleoni, 1975, p. 58)

Smith is therefore significant because, standing at the threshold of industrial capitalism, he captured its essential form, and in writing this form constituted modern economic theory. Two divergent objections can however be sustained against such a contention: firstly, 'modern economic analysis' was founded in the work of Malthus, Ricardo, Mill, and McCulloch, which, forty years after the first publication of *The Wealth of Nations*, used this text to argue out principles which departed radically from the text of 1776, at the same time using it to establish an orthodoxy. Secondly, if a form of capitalist economy is to be associated with the period of formation of economic theory, then it is *agrarian* and not *industrial* production which is at issue. To place Smith in the midst of industrial capitalist advance is to subscribe to the erroneous periodisation of an 'Industrial Revolution' around the existence of forms of technology, a periodisation which results in industrial capitalism as a form of organisation of significant sectors of the economy emerging around sixty-five years too soon (in 1760 rather than 1825). It can be suggested that while Classical Political Economy does present an analysis of a capitalist economy, it is the specific structure of capitalist agricultural production which is of relevance. If there *are* theorists who stand at the threshold of industrial capitalist advance, the names are the unfashionable ones of Whately, Senior, and Longfield.

While there are differences between the approaches of

Hollander and Napoleoni, the common source of their approach is the methodology of the history of ideas. This provides a definite limit to the manner in which the 'economics' of Smith can be appraised, be it from a semi-Marxist position as with Napoleoni, or from a neo-classical one as with Hollander.

Up to this point the terms 'Smith', '*The Wealth of Nations*' and 'Smith's economics' have been used interchangeably to designate in a general fashion a body of writing. Such a usage is of course largely a matter of convenience, but the publication in 1976 of the first two parts of a complete and authoritative edition of Smith's works and correspondence forces a closer look at the easy unities presumed in this practice. If a comparison is made with Ricardo, the problem can be more easily appreciated. The definitive edition of Ricardo's works and correspondence comprises nine substantive volumes and one of miscellaneous fragments. These divide into his *Principles*, a volume of his notes on Malthus' *Principles*, two volumes of pamphlets and papers, a volume of Parliamentary speeches and evidence before Parliamentary committees, and four volumes of letters devoted almost exclusively to issues of economic theory and policy. The form of such a collected works therefore in this case renders synonymous 'Ricardo' with 'Ricardo's economics'. But this is not the case with Smith, for already published are *The Theory of Moral Sentiments* and *The Wealth of Nations*, to be followed by his essay on astronomy, his lectures on rhetoric and belles lettres, and his essay on the formation of languages. The correspondence which is due to be published later includes little of direct relation to his 'economics', if the letters already published by Scott are anything to go by (Scott, 1937, pp. 232-314). As has been suggested before when dealing with Hollander, the orthodox approach has been to virtually ignore the existence of Smith's 'other writings' when dealing with 'his economics', while treating only Books One and Two of *The Wealth of Nations* as the appropriate source. The editors of this new edition on the other hand quite correctly draw the attention of the reader to the wide scope of Smith's work, and suggest ways in which this can begin to be appreciated. And it must be emphasised that the thoroughness with which this new edition is edited should at least discourage easy and speculative 'comparisons' between the writings of Smith and his contemporaries and forebears, the scholarly apparatus delineating clearly the possibilities and limits of external reference.

The manner in which the Introduction deals with these problems is however in *The Wealth of Nations* not without its problems. Instead of attempting to demarcate Smith's 'economics' along new lines, the problem is sidestepped via the introduction of a 'philosophical context' which informs the structure of *The Wealth of Nations*. The problem with this 'context' is that it simply comes *first* in the exposition, and is *succeeded* by a more or less orthodox appraisal of the economic content of *The Wealth of Nations* which only relates marginally to the proposed context. The declared aim of broadening an appreciation of the work of Smith is thereby expressed in a *succession* of dimensions which in overall terms does little to dislodge the isolation of an 'economic' Smith from a 'moral philosopher' Smith.

In recent years however a different basis has emerged on which the work of Smith might be unified; this is the so-called 'four-stages' theory of historical development, in which human history is periodised into successive stages of forms of subsistence (hunting, pastoralism, agriculture, and commerce). This conception is to be found in its first published form in Dalrymple's *Essay Towards a General History of Feudal Property in Great Britain* (1757), although there are grounds for arguing that Smith formulated the notion before this date (Meek, 1976, pp. 99ff.). It is notable however that Meek takes as his major source for Smith the lecture notes of 1762–3[5] and not sections of *The Wealth of Nations*. The point at which the kind of arguments that Smith puts forward in his lectures might be expected to emerge in the later book is in those sections dealing with differing systems of land tenure, where the notion of historical stages could elucidate specific differences in property forms. But in these sections, such as Book One, Chapter XI ('Of the Rent of Land') the argument is confined to the relations of landlord and tenant, and the relation of the rent to the product. References to 'earlier stages', of which perhaps the most memorable is the beaver–deer exchange in Book One Chapter VI, are not the truncated remnants of a historical-philosophical project, but are simply illustrative devices. The Classical Political Economists later used a similar device in postulating an earlier state of society to better emphasise the structure of the present.

Meek's use of the four-stages argument enables him to argue decisively against those who constitute Smith as a precocious neo-classicist, but the extent to which this philosophical history functions in *The Wealth of Nations* can be questioned. In fact, this periodisation of history according to the forms of subsistence treats the property forms in which this subsistence activity occurs as secondary, and so makes problematic the insertion of a philosophy of history into the exposition of an economic discourse.

What, though, is the specificity of this 'economics' that Smith advances? To begin to answer this problem, it is necessary to provide a brief outline of what is generally known as 'eighteenth-century economics', or, as it will be referred to here, 'Political Oeconomy'.

In earlier sections of this essay reference has been made to an 'economic archive' as an alternative formulation to the more usual 'eighteenth-century economics'. This usage is quite deliberate, and is fundamental to the argument that is being made concerning the form of organisation of histories of economics. For as was shown with respect to Hollander's treatment of a collection of 'Pre-Smithian economists', it is always a principle of recurrence which constitutes a series of texts into a unity and treats them as precursors to, or anticipators of, a theoretical structure which they themselves were not part of. This practice can only be regarded as 'historical' insofar as a series of statement are located as preceding the theory which is deployed to nominate them as part of its genesis. Strictly speaking, therefore, these histories are anachronistic, for the criteria by which past statements are judged are always those formed in later discourses. The interest which such histories show in chronology simply hides this basic technique.

This criticism does not imply however that the solution to this problem is 'real history', for that would merely compound the historicism of anachronistic histories. To dispose of such an approach altogether requires that alternative means are formulated which enable 'archival discourses' to be treated with rather more respect. The first move in any such appraisal is to remove the bland phrases ('mercantilism', 'eighteenth-century economics', 'bullionism' and so on) that serve to constitute the unities bandied about in the world of the history of ideas. The texts can then be returned to the archives, and space has been cleared for a fresh start, in which analysis of archival discourses is no longer always looking over its shoulder to see where it is going.

Political Oeconomy is the characteristic form of economic discourse in the seventeenth and eighteenth centuries, a discourse that includes in its sweep those areas normally referred to as mercantilism and political arithmetic, as well as writing not normally considered within the province of 'economic thought'. This distinct discursive unity is characterised by the conception of the national economy as a vast household. The Greek spelling therefore designates a concept quite distinct from the usual notion of 'economy', since the form of organisation is that of householding rather than of production and distribution, and furthermore to function requires the guidance of a patriarchal Statesman. Perhaps the most systematic exposition of this can be found in Steuart's *Inquiry into the Principles of Political Oeconomy* (1767):

> Oeconomy, in general, is the art of providing for all the wants of a family, with prudence and frugality.
>
> If any thing necessary or useful be found wanting, if any thing provided be lost or misapplied, if any servant, any animal, be supernumery or useless, if any one sick or infirm be neglected, we immediately perceive a want of oeconomy. The object of it, in a private family, is therefore to provide for the nourishment, the other wants, and the employment of every individual. In the first place, for the master, who is the head, and who directs the whole; next for the children, who interest him above all other things; and last for the servants, who being useful to the head, and essential to the well-being of the family, have therefore a title to become an object of the master's care and concern.
>
> The whole oeconomy must be directed by the head, who is both lord and steward of the family. (Steuart, 1966, p. 15)

This model of the household is then deployed by Steuart to formulate the organisation of the state or polity, and it is worth quoting further the manner in which this is argued:

> What oeconomy is in the family, political oeconomy is in a

> state: with these essential differences, however, that in a state there are no servants, all are children: that a family may be formed when and how a man pleases, and he may there establish what plan of oeconomy he thinks fit; but states are found formed, and the oeconomy of these depends on a thousand circumstances. The *statesman* (this is a general term to signify the legislature and supreme power, according to the form of government) is neither master to establish what oeconomy he pleases, or, in the exercise of his supreme authority, to overturn at will the established laws of it, let him be the most despotic monarch on earth.
>
> The great art therefore of political oeconomy is, first to adapt the different operations of it to the spirit, manners, habits, and customs of the people; and afterwards to model these circumstances so as to be able to introduce a set of new and more useful institutions.
>
> The principal object of this science is to secure a certain fund of subsistence for all the inhabitants, to obviate every circumstance which may render it precarious; to provide every thing necessary for supplying the wants of the society, and to employ the inhabitants (supposing them to be free men) in such a manner as naturally to create reciprocal relations and dependencies between them, so as to make their several interests lead them to supply one another with their reciprocal wants. (Steuart, 1966, pp. 16–17)

Note that this delination provides no specific theoretical object for this 'science' other than a series of practical branches and areas of administration, which had already been enumerated by Steuart in the Preface as 'population, agriculture, trade, industry, money, coin, interest, circulation, banks, exchange, public credit, and taxes' (Steuart, 1966, p. 7). These categories, comprising institutions, forms of exchange, and regions of an economy, are presented in no specific order, for in Political Oeconomy their pertinence only takes shape with respect to state policy. Expressing the possible variations of writing in this discursive structure, these terms simply *designate* economic spheres, and must not be regarded as concepts in the order of a theoretical structure. This taxonomical nature of Political Oeconomy is one of the major characteristics which differentiates clearly from those discourses which employ the 'same words', most notably Classical Political Economy. The relation of the elements of Political Oeconomy is not established via the properties of the categories, but they take their place according to their function in a system of circulation.

The Sovereign or Statesman is essential in the structure of this discourse, since in his administration of an aggregated 'polity' he is the sole expression of a unity which is otherwise dispersed among individual units or the categories which articulate these units. The 'individual' unit of administration is in this conception the *family*, ruled by a patriarchal figure in a fashion analogous to that of the state:

> The great object of policy, therefore, with respect to both [population and national wealth], is, to secure the family its means of subsistence and settlement; to protect the industrious in the pursuit of his occupation; to reconcile the restrictions of police, and the social affections of mankind, with their separate and interested pursuits. (Ferguson, 1966, pp. 143–4)

While composed in this way of family households, the polity can be divided in several ways, for example by sector (trade, manufacture, agriculture) or by consumption (productive versus unproductive populations). Much of the debate which takes place considers first the relative merits of such elements, and then discusses how these incorporate into the polity and thus become objects for the administration of the Statesman. There are two categories which permit the formulation of this: taxation and money. The first is the means by which the Statesman intervenes to both support and order the 'economy', and the second is the means by which comparisons of the different elements in the polity can be affected via a common standard. This concentration on money and taxation then in turn leads to a conception of the economy as a system of *circulation* of goods and money, in which 'growth' should be understood as the augmentation of this circulation. It is in this framework that discussions of the relative roles of trade and agriculture in contributing to the national strength are placed.

The order of discourse dictates the form in which the 'economy' is represented; and empirical reference to the structure of the economy must find a place within this discursive structure in order to be expressed. There are of course a number of ways within which this occurs, from the numerical arguments of Gregory King and William Petty, to the formulations of Hume. It is not possible here to pursue any further the investigation of Political Oeconomy, but it should be clear from the summary given that it is possible to elaborate an analysis which does not rely on the work of Smith or any other body of economic theory in order to constitute it. The outline that has been given should be sufficient to note that the critique that Smith made of 'mercantilism' in Book Four of *The Wealth of Nations* provides a specific representation of a set of 'predecessors' in which the principle of unity is to be located in the discourse of Smith rather than the alleged 'mercantilists'.

So far we have provisionally treated *The Wealth of Nations* as the locus of Smith's 'economics' without effectively questioning its relation (or lack of it) to *The Theory of Moral Sentiments*. While there is quite clearly a divergence of object between the two texts, a consideration of any connection between them will help elucidate the exact nature of Smith's version of economic analysis.

Dugald Stewart in his appreciation of Smith summed up the *Theory* as follows:

> The fundamental principle of Mr. Smith's theory is, that the primary object of our moral perceptions are the actions of other men; and that our moral judgements with respect to our own conduct are only applications to ourselves of decisions which we have already passed on the conduct of our neighbour. (Stewart, 1811, p. 23)

This last statement captures the Smithian notion of 'sympathy', located as the inter-subjective nature of understanding. This provides the social order with its rationality, for the combined fellow-feeling of the members of a society contrives to produce a harmony that is not the outcome of intentional action. 'Justice' for example is located in this idea of sympathy, since the conception of self-interest can only be formulated *via* the general interests of mankind. It is curious that the proposed relationship here between the ego and the social is analogous to the conception of economic action constructed in neo-classical economics; curious because this intersubjectivity is displaced from *The Wealth of Nations*. Instead, economic man is transposed into this text from the late nineteenth century.

This conception of sympathy leads to the introduction by Smith of the idea of an 'invisible hand' guiding the individual interests into a natural harmony. In the *Theory*, this idea occurs in the discussion of rich and poor in society:

> The rich only select from the heap what is most precious and agreeable. They consume little more than the poor, and in spite of their natural selfishness and rapacity, though they mean only their own conveniency, though the sole end which they propose from the labours of all the thousands whom they employ, be the gratification of their own vain and insatiable desires, they divide with the poor the produce of all their improvements. They are led by an invisible hand to make nearly the same distribution of the necessaries of life, which would have been made, had the earth been divided into equal portions among all its inhabitants, and thus without intending it, without knowing it, advance the interest of society, and afford means to the multiplication of the species. When providence divided the earth among a few lordly masters, it neither forgot nor abandoned those who seem to have been left out in the partition. These last too enjoy their share of all that it produces. In what constitutes the real happiness of human life, they are in no respect inferior to those who would seem so much above them. In ease of body and peace of mind, all the different ranks of life are nearly upon a level, and the beggar, who suns himself by the side of the highway, possesses that security which kings are fighting for.
>
> (*TMS*, pp. 184-5)

This passage has been quoted at length because it brings out sharply the conception of a natural harmony of society in which difference conspires to regulate the social order, rather than disrupt it. The mechanism which reunites the diverse interests, which over-rides the subjective calculation of action, is the calculation of this action by an ego who has sympathy with other egos. The invisible hand of intersubjectivity ensures the harmonious working of the whole.

The conception of the autonomous harmonisation of the social order is central to *The Wealth of Nations*, where an aggregate of calculating 'sympathetic' individuals is co-ordinated in a moral economy. The invisible hand is here the principle of unity among a collection of divided individuals. But what must be emphasised is that the *autonomy* of the invisible hand is the object of the earlier sections of this text, and not the behaviour of economic agents, be they individuals or enterprises. It was for this reason that the remark was made above concerning the importation by neo-classicism of a later nineteenth-century creation to 'put Smith straight'.

The common principle uniting the individuals in *The Wealth of Nations* is not a proclivity to fellow-feeling: it is instead *labour*, which constitutes the wealth of a nation:

> The annual labour of every nation is the fund which originally supplies it with all the necessaries and conveniences of life which it annually consumes, and which consist always, either in the immediate produce of that labour, or in what is purchased with that produce from other nations.
>
> (*WN*, p. 10)

This 'original fund' is one of aggregated human labour, establishing the anthropological basis of the conception of wealth that it founds. Consequently, having stated this in the opening paragraph of the Introduction, Smith turns to the population among which this wealth is divided, and following on from this, the proportion of this population engaged in useful labour. The importance of dividing up the population in this fashion soon becomes apparent:

> Whatever be the actual state of the skill, dexterity, and judgement with which labour is applied in any nation, the abundance of scantiness of its annual supply must depend, during the continuance of that state, upon the proportion between the number of those who are annually employed in useful labour, and that of those who are not so employed. The number of useful and productive labourers, it will hereafter appear, is every where in proportion to the quantity of capital stock which is employed in setting them to work, and to the particular way in which it is so employed.
>
> (*WN*, p. 11)

The productive/unproductive distinction serves to formulate the 'capital stock' of a nation. Unlike the earlier usage of Petty, D'Avenant and King, where the distinction serves to identify useful *sectors* of employment of forms of income, the notion of a *form of labour* is used to discriminate among the population of a nation. Labour thus is crucially related to Smith's notion of capital, or rather, productive labour is constitutive of capital stock. The extensive use that Smith makes of this productive/unproductive formula is dictated by this need to formulate a concept of capital which is something other than a simple accumulation of 'wealth' as bullion or goods. The wealth of a nation is its productive labour; to ask of Smith, 'productive of what?' in the manner that Marx did is to misrecognise the strictly limited discursive function that this notion fulfils.

The form in which this 'capital stock' accumulates is expressed in the development of the division of labour, for as the stock accumulates the division of labour, conceived as the distribution of technical skills, becomes more complex. The examples that Smith advances demonstrate however that this is thought only with respect to individual enterprises (*WN*, Chs I–III Bk One); and indeed, the celebrated example of the pin factory concerns the manufacture of products based entirely on handwork, such that it is clear that this division of labour is between persons and not inscribed in the organisation of a productive process. There is no example in Smith which deals with the relationship of enterprises to each other in the development of a division of labour. The reason for this is simple: the dynamic of economic action is self-interest, and the rule of the invisible hand extends only to the regulation of the wills of conscious subjects. Enterprises cannot have wills, or rather, can only be possessed of wills through identification with a capitalist.

It should be clear then that it is possible to deal with Smith's usage of division of labour independently of any direct reference to contemporary industrial practices. The functioning of this term must be grasped not in its correspondence with 'real factories' (as Hollander argues) but rather as a concept which is implicated in a matrix with other concepts, forms of proof, and forms of explanation. To clarify this point, it is worth distinguishing the use of the concept 'divison of labour' in *The Wealth of Nations* from its use in two other eighteenth-century texts, Ferguson's *On the History of Civil Society* (1767), and Hume's *Treatise of Human Nature* (1739–40).

In the fourth part of Ferguson's essay ('Of Consequences that Result from the Advancement of Civil and Commercial Arts') there is to be found a discussion of a division of labour that has been regarded as analogous to that of Smith, and furthermore this instance supposedly formed the basis for a dispute between Smith and Ferguson on priority (Hamowy, 1968, pp. 249–50). The most concise statement of this is as follows:

> Every undertaker in manufacture finds, that the more he can subdivide the tasks of his workmen, and the more hands he can employ on separate articles, the more are his expenses diminished, and his profits increased. The consumer, too, requires, in every kind of commodity, a workmanship more perfect that hands employed on a variety of subjects can produce, and the progress of commerce is but a continued subdivision of the mechanical arts.
>
> (Ferguson, 1966, p. 181)

The progressive division of skills is here seen as the basis for the advance of society, conceived as another dimension of the development of civil society. Elsewhere in this essay Ferguson has considered human nature, individual and national sentiments, monarchy and other forms of political order, population, national defence and conquest; all of these items being organised according to their contribution to the effective functioning of civil society. Thus the conception of division of labour functions here with respect to the progress of a social order:

> By the separation of arts and professions, the sources of wealth are laid open; every species of material is wrought up to the greatest perfection, and every commodity is produced in the greatest abundance. The state may estimate its profits and its revenues by the number of its people.
>
> (Ferguson, 1966, p. 181)

Unlike *The Wealth of Nations*, the conception of division of labour is conceived according to a schema of social progress. The crucial link to the form of accumulation of a capital stock, constituting the wealth of a nation, is entirely absent. Again, the object of Ferguson's essay is to elaborate the conditions for general progress of the social order, an enterprise distinct from that of Smith.

If we turn to Hume and his use of 'division of labour' it can also be easily shown that this is a distinct concept from the one employed by Smith, despite claims to the contrary (Hamowy, 1968, p. 251). Part Two of Book Three of the *Treatise* deals with justice and injustice, and in doing so introduces some remarks on the natural state of man and animals. He argues that man has been ill supplied by nature with the means to relieve the numerous necessities that have also been prescribed. Unlike the animals, man in himself has a disproportion between his wants and his advantages. The solution to this dilemma is proposed by Hume as follows:

> 'Tis by society alone he is able to supply his defects, and raise himself up to an equality with his fellow-creatures, and even acquire a superiority above them. By society all his infirmities are compensated; and tho' in that situation his wants multiply every moment upon him, yet his abilities are still more augmented, and leave him in every respect more satisfied and happy, than 'tis possible for him, in his savage and solitary condition, ever to become. When every individual labours a-part, and only for himself, his force is too small to execute any considerable work, his labour being employ'd in supplying all his different necessities, he never attains a perfection in any particular art; and as his force and success are not at all times equal, the least failure in either of these particulars must be attended with inevitable ruin and misery. Society provides a remedy for these *three* inconveniences. By the conjunction of forces, our power is augmented: By the partition of employments, our ability encreases: And by mutual succour we are less expos'd to fortune and accidents. 'Tis by this additional *force*, *ability*, and *security*, that society becomes advantageous. (Hume, 1898 Vol. II, p. 259)

Thus the combination and co-operation of men in society compensates for their disability, compared with animals, in a natural state. The distinction of man from animal is located in this ability to form a social order, and in so doing man lays a basis for his progress. The notion of 'division of labour' introduced here is simply that the social collectivity through co-operation can effect more than the individual separated from such a collectivity. As in Ferguson, it is the social order which is at issue; but the difference here is that 'division' is merely the basis of its existence. Just as in Ferguson, it is only in the most banal sense that it could be said that Smith, Ferguson, and Hume shared a concept of the division of labour. Reduced to this banality, it is no longer possible to specify the exact nature of the concept in *The Wealth of Nations*. Accordingly, attention has been focused on the specific concept deployed in Smith's text, rather than an 'idea of the Scottish Enlightenment'.

The object for Smith is not a social order and its progress, but rather an economic order and its progress. He constitutes the economy as a collection of rational subjects, whose economising activity leads to greater productivity and thereby accumulation of the capital stock. In this conception the conditions of existence of the enterprises in which this activity proceeds can only be established through *policy*, which is the province of the administrator of the economy.

As might be expected, the notion of value that emerges in this argument is an anthropological one, for labour is treated as the 'real measure':

> Every man is rich or poor according to the degree in which he can afford to enjoy the necessaries, conveniencies, and amusements of human life. But after the division of labour has once thoroughly taken place, it is but a very small part of these with which a man's own labour can supply him. The far greater part of them he must derive from the labour of other people, and he must be rich or poor according to the quantity of that labour which he can command, or which he can afford to purchase. The value of any commodity, therefore, to the person who possesses it, and who means not to use or consume it himself, but to exchange if for other commodities, is equal to the quantity of labour which it enables him to purchase or command. Labour, therefore, is the real measure of the exchangeable value of all commodities. (*WN*, p. 47)

'Value' therefore is the outcome of the calculation of sympathetic individuals; and because of this, a divergence appears between the nominal price of labour, and the real price which is established independently of these calculating individuals. Again, it can be seen from the passage above how the conception(s) of value in Smith relate closely to the already-elaborated notion of the division of labour, providing the basis for exchange between differentiated elements. The nature of value in *The Wealth of Nations* will however be discussed in more detail below.

The remarks made so far have been addressed to various sections of Book One of *The Wealth of Nations*, and while it is not the intention here to proceed in this fashion through the entire text, some comments can be made on what is virtually 'unknown territory' to neo-classicism, ie. Books Three, Four and Five. But even in the most 'modern' section of the text, that which is identified by neo-classicism as its precursor and foundation, there are some deeply embedded forms which relate directly to the discourse of Political Oeconomy. Even a cursory treatment of the later sections serves to underline this.

Those readers of the Penguin edition of Smith's text will probably be baffled by the content of Book Three, apparently unrelated as it is to the theory of the firm, international trade, money, general equilibrium and all the other neo-classical 'finds' of Book One and Two. Dealing as it does with the relation of agriculture and commerce, it examines the different relations between town and country, and the effect of one or the other's preponderance on the wealth of a national economy. Through all the diverse historical arguments that are cited in these chapters runs a clear conception of agriculture as the naturally prior concern of a national economy, with the rise of commerce only being beneficial insofar as agriculture is unhindered in its progress. In this fashion the argument of Book Four is prefigured, for here it is that Smith counterposes two principle systems in Political Oeconomy: the 'mercantilists' and the 'agriculturalists'.

In dealing with the former Smith reviews the areas of 'policy' pertinent to the well-being of the economy, such as bounties, drawbacks and tariffs, and poses in the chapters dealing with such questions the suitability of these as instruments of the administration of an economy. For example, Chapter VII of Book Four examines the benefits and drawbacks of colonies, and their effects on the rise of monopolies. In promoting such a rise, he concludes, the improvement of land is discouraged, owing to the raised rate of mercantile profit (*WN*, pp. 604–13). The 'mercantilists' are those who favour such commercial policy; against them Smith poses the Physiocrats, who with their agrarian conception of the national economy are dealt with very sympathetically. While arguing that this system erroneously treats 'artificers, manufacturers and merchants, as altogether barren and unproductive' (*WN*, p. 674), he in general endorses its arguments concerning wealth, profit and labour. And in doing this, *The Wealth of Nations* departs even more radically from the model text which provides the first analysis of industrial capitalism.

Book Five considers the revenues necessary for the proper exercise of state functions, and in developing this a familiar figure appears: the Statesman, usually omitted from modern discussions of Smith principally because the construction made of *The Wealth of Nations* does not allow for this strange 'residue' of the eighteenth century. Having established the economy as a self-regulating collectivity of sympathetic subjects in Books One and Two, Smith can argue that it can do for itself whatever is necessary more effectively than a patriarchal statesman could. But at the end of Book Four we encounter a Sovereign with quite specific duties, which although limited in their scope, retain the place of the Statesman (*WN*, p. 687). Three duties are given to the statesman: first, the defence of the society against other societies; second, the protection of individual members of the society from injustice; and third, to establish and maintain the public works which no individual would undertake. Despite these serious limitations on the power of a statesman, the argument of Book Five deals with taxation and revenue in a manner customary in the eighteenth century, recapitulating the polity by tracing the course of monetary circulation. It must be emphasised that the system of self-regulation in the earlier parts of the text concern the self-regulation of a system of *circulation*, the natural object of Political Oeconomy.

It cannot be claimed that Smith breaks decisively with Political Oeconomy, for while he in some ways undermines it he continues its form in others. Smith did not found Classical Political Economy in *The Wealth of Nations*: he provided the classical economists with the text that became the foundation of economic discourse. In the same way that Smith created his precursors in the critique of 'mercantilism', so *The Wealth of Nations* is canonised as the precursor of Classical Political Economy in the writings of Malthus and Ricardo.

Writing which addressed itself to discussion of the national economy was until the early nineteenth century heavily influenced by the work of the Physiocrats, or, as they were known, the 'Agriculturalists'. It was the opposition to this current that first systematically introduced reference to *The Wealth of Nations*, constituting this text as a work of orthodoxy, a position to be held for much of the nineteenth century. It is notable that in this early guise the text was deployed against the body of theory that had been approved of in Book Four. However, the orthodoxy of the 1820s, the 'high phase' of Classical Political Economy, was a diverse one, nominally oriented around the Ricardians in the one hand, and the 'Smithians' on the other. Both McCulloch and Malthus were counted in the ranks of the latter, although they were themselves bitterly divided. The position that *The Wealth of Nations* occupied in this discursive formation can perhaps in conclusion be briefly outlined by introducing some remarks on the notion of 'value'.

The definitions and re-definitions of 'value' practically without exception took their point of departure from the formulations of Smith. Unfortunately this was not without its problems, since Smith produced a theory based on subjective estimation and also one based on labour time. Ricardo in Chapter 1 of his *Principles* rejected the first and developed the second. But in this process of development two things occurred: firstly, the concept of value became derivative of a *matrix* of commodities, such that if the value of one changed then all the others did; and secondly, progressively more attention was paid to the problem of an invariant measure of value. It was this last problem that was being worked over at the time of his death, and the results of his analysis can be seen in the draft and partially completed manuscript 'Absolute and Exchangeable Value' (Ricardo IV, 1951, pp. 357–412). The issues which this raised was the subject of much discussion between Malthus, McCulloch and Ricardo, the bases of which are difficult to disentangle given the natural confusion in the writings of the first two writers.[6]

Malthus in the first edition of his *Principles* for example argued as follows:

> That a correct measure of real value in exchange would be very desirable cannot be doubted, as it would at once enable us to form a just estimate and comparison of wages, incomes, and

> commodities, in all countries and at all periods; but when we consider what a measure of real value in exchange implies, we shall feel doubtful whether any one commodity exists, or can easily be supposed to exist, with such properties, as would qualify it to become a standard measure of this kind. Whatever article, or even mass of articles, we refer to, must itself be subject to change; and all that we can hope for is an approximation to the measure which is the object of our search.
>
> (Malthus, 1820, p. 60)

The dilemma faced by Malthus was one which occupied other classical theorists, for what they in fact were doing was extracting certain elements from the body of *The Wealth of Nations* and attempting to systematically link them together. In Smith, value (in both his senses) is thought of with respect to a collectivity of rationalising subjects, the population of a national economy ruled by an invisible hand. The exposition of his concepts is intricately related to such a project. Classical Political Economy does away with this, more or less successfully. In the case of Malthus, less successfully: for the concept of value cannot be regarded as the object of theoretical research in the manner of Ricardo, but has to be related to a concrete origin. Accordingly in Malthus the *measure* of value often is thought of as the *origin* of value. In his earlier writings therefore the variability of labour leads him to average it with corn, producing a corn/labour standard on the basis of the dubious reasoning that they vary inversely in real conditions (Malthus, 1820, pp. 127, 128–9).

Ricardo, in departing from Smith, was not interested in value as the principle for the equal exchange between differentiated individuals, but rather as the means for theorising the relation between wages, profits and rents, and their distribution to landlords, capitalist and labourers (Ricardo I, 1951, p. 29). In so doing he abandoned the 'subjective' form of Smith's value theory, and attempted to develop the notion of labour as measure. His comments on Malthus' *Principles of Political Economy* illustrate this:

> In all that Mr. M. has yet said about exchangeable value, it appears to depend a great deal on the wants of mankind, and the relative estimation in which they hold commodities. This would be true if men from various countries were to meet in

> a fair, with a variety of productions, and each with a separate commodity, undisturbed by the competition of any other seller. Commodities, under such circumstances, would be bought and sold according to the relative wants of those attending the fair – but when the wants of society are well known, when there are hundreds of competitors who are willing to satisfy those wants, on the condition only that they shall have the known and usual profits, there can be no such rule for regulating the value of commodities.
>
> (Ricardo II, 1951, pp. 24–5)

The problem of the regulation of value coincides with the more abstract problem of the measure of value: for if there is a unique and unchanging measure of value than this problem is disposed of.

But Ricardo refused to allow that labour could be such an invariant measure, and when Malthus published his *Measure of Value Stated and Illustrated* in 1823 he criticised Malthus for choosing 'a variable measure for an invariable standard' (Ricardo to Malthus, 29 April 1823; Ricardo IX, 1952, p. 282). In so doing Malthus had avowedly returned to the work of Smith, although he claimed to have done so by a circuitous route (Malthus, 1823, p. v). Ricardo in his correspondence with Mill and McCulloch at this period made clear his allegiance to a conception of commodity value based on comparative quantities of labour bestowed in production, rejecting both Smith's conception of 'estimation' and also of cost of production.

One of the more well-known critiques of the position that Ricardo adopted is that of Bailey, who argued that Smith's definition of value as the power of purchasing other goods was substantially correct (Bailey, 1825, p. 4). He located the problem of variability of any measure as a handicap to Ricardo's approach to value, and further suggested that:

> It has been taken for granted that we measure value as we measure extension, or ascertain weight; and it has been consequently imagined, that to perform the operation we must possess an object of invariable value.
>
> (Bailey, 1825, pp. 95–6)

While it may be questioned how far such a criticism bears on the Ricardian formulation, the principal concern here is the way in which again it is with respect to the text of Smith that the positions are marked out. The arguments among the Classical Economists concerning the nature and measure of value depended crucially on the work of Smith, insofar as it represented a series of positions that could be worked and reworked. It is also notable that even here in the early nineteenth century it is Books One and Two that are the subject of discussion. No longer is the administration of a state central to the constitution of an object of discourse. Where Ricardo presents his formulations concerning taxation, these are conceived not as matters of direct policy but rather as the incidence of forms of taxation on a commercial economy – which is not the same as 'the English nation'.

Economic theory constitutes a knowledge of 'economic processes'. But the economic process is not a pre-given object, to which theory is more or less adequate. As we have seen, Political Oeconomy constituted production as a phase of a process of circulation. In this way, capitalist industrial production was dealt with as equivalent to trading ventures, the only difference being that it continually augments the process of circulation. This cannot be said to be an illusion, an ideological form which concealed the real working of the economy from its agents. The conception of augmented circulation can be found in the forms of accounting of early enterprises, and other conceptions of organisation – so Political Oeconomy is not just a set of ideas, it has material forms and effects.

One of the principal distinguishing features which marks that discursive formation referred to here as 'Classical Political Economy' is that it developed a different conception of the economic process in attempting to deal with the structure of agrarian capitalist production. In so doing, a decisive break was made with those works which at the same time were treated as standard texts. The principal work of such a nature, *The Wealth of Nations*, occupies an indeterminate position within this process, undermining the bases of Political Oeconomy but at the same time remaining within its confines. The work of Ricardo, Malthus and the others was to rewrite Smith out of this dilemma.

Accordingly, this essay has attempted to deal with two related problems. The first is the general one concerning the mode of organisation of the history of ideas, in this case represented by the history of economics. It was argued that through the confusion of the object of a history with that of the object of theoretical discourse a series of problems arise which vitiate the analysis of sectors of the economic archive. The second problem concerned the manner in which the histories of economics have nominated *The Wealth of Nations* as the founding moment of modern economic theory. This canonisation depends however on the suitability of the text in question as a vehicle of contemporary theory. This activity of recurrence in present-day historians has a respectable predecessor in the activity of the economists of the early nineteenth century, who themselves began the tradition of originating economic discourse in *The Wealth of Nations*. The object of historical work is however not the same as the object of theoretical work, and such an approach, while acceptable in the latter, is suspect in the former.

Notes

NOTES TO CHAPTER 1

1. There is not space here to discuss the various problems of 'feudalism' as a category, but reference can be made to the discussions in Bloch (1963) and Brown (1974); and to Cahen (1977) and Müller-Mertens (1977) for its use in Marxist historical work. In addition, it must be noted that an extensive debate on the nature of feudalism and the question of transition has gone on in the Soviet Union since the 1930s – see for example Wädekin (1952), Baron (1972) and Goehrke (1974).
2. Marx used the opposition 'bourgeoisie' and 'proletariat' in the *Communist Manifesto* as a form of power relation in modern society not related in the first instance to economic categories. It was only with the development of an analysis of the capitalist mode of production that the 'two classes' become effectively realised as economic categories.
3. This has been shown for instance in Brown's examination of the nature of 'historical materialism' as manifested in Engels' *Origin of the Family* (Brown, 1979, pp. 9, 18–19).

NOTES TO CHAPTER 2

1. Brides received cash and/or land as a dowry to take with them, while wives were assigned land in exchange to secure them against the chance of their husbands predeceasing them, in which event the estate would pass beyond their generation to the next.
2. 'Assarting' is the clearing and cultivation of waste land.
3. Titow expressed disagreement with Thirsk's characterisation of the elements of a common-field system, and proposed that no meaningful distinction could be made between 'open' and 'common' fields (1965). Baker later suggested that the term 'open' field should be abandoned altogether (1969, p. 140).
4. Leases for lives secured the tenant for long periods, calculated in life-spans, in exchange for a high entry fine and low subsequent annual rents. 'At will' did away with this system for the sake of greater control over the rental revenue, which could be more easily raised with improvement or higher product prices. Of course, the absence of a large irregu-

lar fine income was more readily noticed than the improved yearly flow of adjustable rentals.

5. Hueckel discusses similar problems in the estimation of farm capital and profitability in his article on the Napoleonic period (1976).

NOTES TO CHAPTER 3

1. Blanqui's book appeared in German translation in 1840–1, but in the present editions of Engels' text there is no direct indication of his acquaintance with Blanqui's book in either French or German version.
2. The problem of the terminology of the 'Industrial Revolution' was brought to my attention by Tine Bruland's paper, 'The Historiography of the Industrial Revolution'.

NOTES TO CHAPTER 4

1. The chronology of the history of economics is based on:
   1. the life span of an author;
   2. the dating of texts;
   3. the dating of citations given in texts and their genesis;
   4. the dating of predecessors.

   When combined, these factors provide the basis for differentiating schools, where one of the dominant concerns becomes the ease with which particular writers fit into the unities they are assigned to.
2. See Ch. 1 of Hindess and Hirst (1977). When it is stated that economic thought is expressive of a distinct and material economic order in the 'real world', ie. 'reality determines thought', all that happens is a reference from one privileged discourse (a set of statements describing a given economic structure) to another (a set of statements in the form of theoretical propositions). The 'real' is a construct masquerading as a given truth; but in no way is this to deny the actual existence of a 'real world', rather it is important to be careful of the limitations of arguments which appeal to its existence as a means of establishing priority. Cf. also Tribe (1978).
3. For a discussion of the use of Kuhn and Lakatos in the historiography of economics, see Tribe (1978, Ch. 1)
4. A recent review of the literature can be found in Kindleberger (1976).
5. Now published in *Lectures on Jurisprudence* (Smith, 1978, pp. 1–394).
6. O'Brien in his treatment of McCulloch's treatment of value identifies at least three quite distinct positions which are often found run together in his writings (1970, Ch. 8).

Bibliography

Albert, W. (1972) *The Turnpike Road System in England, 1663–1840,* Cambridge University Press, London.

Anderson, P. (1964) 'Origins of the Present Crisis', *New Left Review*, No. 23, pp. 26–54.

— (1974a) *Passages from Antiquity to Feudalism*, NLB, London.

— (1974b) *Lineages of the Absolutist State,* NLB, London.

Bachelard, G. (1965) *L'Activité rationaliste de la physique contemporaine,* P.U.F., Paris.

Bailey, S. (1825) *A Critical Dissertation on the Nature, Measures, and Causes of Value,* R. Hunter, London.

Baker, A. R. H. (1965) 'Howard Levi Gray and English Field Systems: An Evaluation', *Agricultural History,* Vol. 39, pp. 86–91.

— 'Some Terminological Problems in Studies of British Field Systems', *Agricultural History Review*, Vol. 17 (1969) pp. 136–40.

— and Butlin, R. A. (1973) 'Conclusion: Problems and Perspectives', in Baker and Butlin (eds), *Studies of Field Systems in the British Isles,* Cambridge University Press, London, pp. 619–56.

Baldinger, K. (1963) 'Einige terminologische Auswirkungen des Aufschwungs der Industrie im 18.Jahrhundert in Frankreich', *Alteuropa und die moderne Gesellschaft* (Brunner Festschrift), Vandenhoeck und Ruprecht, Göttingen, pp. 318–35.

Balibar, E. (1970) 'The Basic Concepts of Historical Materialism', in L. Althusser and E. Balibar, *Reading Capital,* NLB, London, pp. 199–308.

Barnes, D. G. (1930) *A History of the English Corn Laws 1600–1846,* George Routledge and Sons, London.

Baron, S. H. (1972) 'The Transition from Feudalism to Capitalism in Russia: A Major Soviet Historical Controversy', *American Historical Review,* Vol. 77, pp. 715-29.

Barrell, J. (1972) *The Idea of Landscape and the Sense of Place 1730–1840,* Cambridge University Press, London.

Barton, J. (1817) *Observations on the Circumstances which Influence the Condition of the Labouring Classes of Society,* J. and A. Arch, London.

Beresford, M. W. (1961) 'Habitation versus Improvement: The Debate on Enclosure by Agreement', in F. J. Fisher (ed.), *Essays in the Economic and Social History of Tudor and Stuart Engalnd,* Cambridge University Press, London, pp. 40-69.

Best, H. (1857) *Rural Economy in Yorkshire in 1641, being the Farming and Account Books of Henry Best of Elmswell, in the East Riding of the County of York,* Surtees Society Vol. 33, George Andrews, Durham.

Bettelheim, C. (1975) *Transition to Socialist Economy,* Harvester, Hassocks.

—— (1976) *Economic Calculation and Forms of Property,* Routledge and Kegan Paul, London.

Bezanson, A. (1922) 'The Early Use of the Term Industrial Revolution', *Quarterly Journal of Economics,* Vol. 36, pp. 343-9.

Blanqui, A. (1837) *Histoire de l'économie politique en Europe,* 2 vols., Guillaumin, Paris.

Blaug, M. (1968) *Economic Theory in Retrospect,* 2nd edition, Heinemann, London.

Bloch, M. (1963) 'European Feudalism', in *Mélanges historiques,* Vol. I, S.E.V:P.E.N., Paris, pp. 177-88.

Bois, G. (1978) 'Against the neo-Malthusian Orthodoxy', *Past and Present,* No. 79, pp. 60-9.

Brenner, R. (1976) 'Agrarian Class Structure and Economic Development in Pre-Industrial Europe', *Past and Present,* No. 70, pp. 30-75.

O'Brien, D. P. (1970) *J. R. McCulloch. A Study in Classical Economics,* George Allen and Unwin, London.

Brown, E. A. R. (1974) 'The Tyranny of a Construct: Feudalism and the Historians of Medieval Europe', *American Historical Review,* Vol. 79, pp. 1063-88.

Brown, L. (1979) 'The Family and its Genealogies – A Discussion of Engels' "The Origin of the Family" ', M/F No. 3, pp. 5-34.

Brunner, O. (1959) *Land und Herrschaft,* Rudolf M. Rohrer, Vienna.

—— (1977) ' "Feudalismus", ein Beitrag zur Begriffsgeschichte', in L. Kuchenbuch and B. Michael (eds), *Feudalismus – Materialen sur Theorie und Geschichte,* Verlag Ullstein, Frankfurt, pp. 155-95.

Buchanan, D. (1814) *Observations on the Subjects Treated of in Dr. Smith's Inquiry into the Nature and Causes of the Wealth of Nations,* Oliphant, Waugh and Innes, Edinburgh.

Burns, E. (1946) 'The Story of Capitalism', *Communist Review,* November, pp. 29-31.

Cahen. C. (1977) Überlegungen zum Gebrauch des Wortes "Feudalismus" ("feodalité")', in L. Kuchenbuch and B. Michael (eds), *Feudalismus – Materialen zur Theorie und Geschichte,* Verlag Ullstein, Frankfurt, pp. 404-19.

Cayley, E. S. (1830) *On Commerical Economy, in Six Essays,* J. Ridgeway, London.

Chambers, J. D. (1947) 'Enclosure and the Small Landowner in Lindsey', *The Lincolnshire Historian,* No. 1, pp. 15-20.

—— (1953) 'Enclosure and Labour Supply in the Industrial Revolution', *Economic History Review*, 2nd series, Vol. 5, pp. 319-43.

—— and Mingay, G. E. (1966) *The Agricultural Revolution 1750-1880*, Batsford, London.

Chartres, J. (1973) 'Markets and Marketing in Metropolitan Western England in the Late Seventeenth and Eighteenth Centuries', in M. Havinden (ed.), *Husbandry and Marketing in the South-West, 1500-1800*, Exeter Papers in Economic History, No. 8, pp. 63-74.

Clapham, J. H. (1923) 'The Growth of an Agrarian Proletariat 1688-1832', *Cambridge Historical Journal,* Vol. 1, pp. 92-5.

—— (1926) *An Economic History of Modern Britain – The Early Railway Age 1820-1850*, Cambridge University Press, London.

Clark, G. de N. (1949) 'On the Great English Revolution', *Communist Review,* May, pp. 523-7.

Clark, G. N. (1970) *The Idea of the Industrial Revolution,* University of Glasgow.

Clay, C. (1966) *Two Families and their Estates: The Grimstons and the Cowpers from c.1650 to c.1815,* PhD thesis, University of Cambridge.
—— (1968) 'Marriage, Inheritance, and the Rise of Large Estates in England, 1600–1815', *Economic History Review,* 2nd series, Vol. 21, pp. 503–18.
Cobbett, W. (1967) *Rural Rides*, Penguin Books, Harmondsworth.
Coleman, J. (1858) 'Farm Accounts' , *Journal of the Royal Agricultural Society of England,* Vol. 19, pp. 122–43.
Collins, E. J. T. (1966) 'Historical Farm Records', *Archives,* Vol. 7, pp. 143–9.
—— (1969) 'Labour Supply and Demand in European Agriculture 1800–1880', in E. L. Jones and S. J. Woolf (eds), *Agrarian Change and Economic Development,* Methuen, London, pp. 61–94.
Collins, K. (1967) 'Marx on the English Agricultural Revolution: Theory and Evidence', *History and Theory,* Vol. 6, pp. 351–81.
Cooper, J. P. (1978) 'In Search of Agrarian Capitalism', *Past Present,* No. 80, pp. 20–65.
Curtler, W. H. R. (1912) 'The Landlords, the Labourers, and the Land', *Economic Review,* Vol. 22, pp. 290–301.
Deane, P. and Cole, W. A. (1962) *British Economic Growth 1688–1959,* Cambridge University Press, London.
Dobb, M. H. (1941) 'The English Revolution', *Labour Monthly,* Vol. 23, No. 2, pp. 92–3.
—— (1963) *Studies in the Development of Capitalism*, Routledge and Kegan Paul, London (First Published 1946).
—— (1967) 'Transition from Feudalism to Capitalism', in *Papers on Capitalism, Development and Planning,* Routledge and Kegan Paul, London, pp. 2–16.
—— (1976) 'A Reply', in R. Hilton (ed.), *The Transition from Feudalism to Capitalism,* NLB, London, pp. 57–67.
Engels, F. (1969) *The Condition of the Working Class in England,* Panther Books, London.
Ernle, Lord (1961) *English Farming, Past and Present,* 6th edition, Heinemann and Frank Cass, London.
Everitt, A. (1968) 'The Food Market of the English Town, 1660–1760', *Third International Conference of Economic History,* Vol. I, Mouton, Paris, pp. 57–71.

Ferguson, A. (1966) *An Essay on the History of Civil Society 1767,* Edinburgh University Press, Edinburgh.

Forbes, F. (1778) *The Improvement of Waste Lands,* N. Conant, London.

Freudenberger, H. and Redlich, F. (1964) 'The Industrial Development of Europe: Reality, Symbols, Images', *Kyklos,* Vol. 17, pp. 372-401.

Fussell, G. E. (ed.) (1936) *Robert Loder's Farm Accounts 1610–1620,* Royal Historical Society, Camden Third Series, Vol. 53.

Garman, D. (1940) 'A Reply to P.F.', *Labour Monthly*, Vol. 22, No. 12, pp. 651–3.

Gaskell, P. (1833) *The Manufacturing Population of England, its Moral, Social, and Physical Conditions, and the Changes which arises from the use of Steam Machinery*, Baldwin & Cradock, London.

Gilboy, E. W. (1934) *Wages in Eighteenth Century England,* Harvard University Press, Cambridge (Mass.).

Goehrke, C. (1974) 'Zum gegenwärtigen Stand der Feudalismus-Diskussion in der Sowjetunion', *Jahrbuch für die Geschichte Osteuropas,* N.F., Vol. 22, pp. 214–47.

Gonner, E. C. K. (1966) *Common Land and Inclosure,* Frank Cass, London.

Gordon, B. (1975) *Economic Analysis before Adam Smith,* Macmillan, London.

Granger, C. W. J. and Elliot, C. M. (1967) 'A Fresh Look at Wheat Prices and Markets in the Eighteenth Century', *Economic History Review*, 2nd series, Vol. 20, pp. 257–65.

Gray, H. L. (1910) 'Yeoman Farming in Oxfordshire from the Sixteenth Century to the Nineteenth', *Quarterly Journal of Economics,* Vol. 24, pp. 293–326.

— (1915) *English Field Systems,* Harvard University Press, Cambridge (Mass.).

Grigg, D. B. (1962a) 'The Development of Tenant Right in South Lincolnshire', *The Lincolnshire Historian,* Vol. 2, pp. 41–8.

— (1962b) 'Changing Regional Values during the Agricultural Revolution in South Lincolnshire', *Transactions and Papers of the Institute of British Geographers,* No. 30, pp. 91–103.

Habakkuk, H. J. (1950) 'Marriage Settlements in the Eighteenth Century', *Transactions of the Royal Historical Society,* 4th series, Vol. 32, pp. 15–30.

—— (1953) 'England', in A. Goodwin (ed.), *The European Nobility in the Eighteenth Century,* Adam and Charles Black, London, pp. 1-21.

—— (1965) 'La disparition du paysan anglais', *Annales,* Vol. 20, pp. 649-63.

Hammond, B. and J. L. (1911) *The Village Labourer 1760-1832,* Longmans, Green and Co., London.

Hamowy, R. (1968) 'Adam Smith, Adam Ferguson, and the Division of Labour', *Economica,* Vol. 35, pp. 249-59.

Harvey, N. (1970) *A History of Farm Buildings in England and Wales,* David and Charles, Newton Abbott.

Harwood Long, W. (1963) 'The Development of Mechanisation in English Farming', *Agricultural History Review,* Vol. 11, pp. 15-26.

Hasbach, W. (1908) *A History of the English Agricultural Labourer,* P. S. King and Son, London.

Hibbert, A. B. (1953) 'The Origins of the Medieval Town Patriciate', *Past and Present,* No. 3, pp. 15-27.

Higgins, J. P. P. and Pollard, S. (eds) (1971) *Aspects of Capital Investment in Great Britain 1750-1850,* Methuen, London.

Hilger, D. (1975) 'Fabrik, Fabrikant', in O. Brunner, W. Conze and R. Koselleck (eds), *Geschichtliche Grundbegriffe* Bd. 2, Ernst Klett Verlag, Stuttgart pp. 229-52.

Hill, C. (1938) 'Soviet Interpretations of the English Interregnum', *Economic History Review,* Vol. 8, pp. 159-67.

—— (1940a) *The English Revolution 1640,* Lawrence and Wishart, London.

—— (1940b) 'The Agrarian Legislation of the Interregnum', *English Historical Review,* Vol. 55, pp. 222-50.

—— (1948a) 'The English Civil War Interpreted by Marx and Engels'. *Science and Society,* Vol. 12, pp. 130-56.

—— (1948b) 'Land in the English Revolution', *Science and Society,* Vol. 13, pp. 22-49.

—— (1950) 'Historians on the Rise of British Capitalism', *Science and Society,* Vol. 14, pp. 307-21.

—— (1976) 'A Comment', in R. Hilton (ed.), *The Transition from Feudalism to Capitalism,* NLB, London, pp. 118-21.

Hilton, R. (1973) *Bond Men Made Free,* Maurice Temple Smith, London.

—— (ed.) (1976a) *The Transition from Feudalism to Capitalism,* NLB, London.

—— (1976b) 'A Comment', in R. Hilton (ed.) *The Transition from Feudalism to Capitalism*, N.L.B., London, pp. 109-17.

—— (1978) 'A Crisis of Feudalism', *Past and Present*, No. 80, pp. 3-19.

Hindess, B. and Hirst, P. Q. (1975) *Pre-Capitalist Modes of Production,* Routledge and Kegan Paul, London.

—— (1977) *Mode of Production and Social Formation*, Macmillan, London.

Hirst, P. Q. (1975) 'The Uniqueness of the West', *Economy and Society,* Vol. 4, pp. 446-75.

Historians' Group, CPGB (1948a) 'Second Session January 10/11 1948', duplicated minutes.

—— (1948b) 'State and Revolution in Tudor and Stuart England', *Communist Review*, July, pp. 207-14.

Hobsbawm E. J. (1954a) 'The General Crisis of the European Economy in the Seventeenth Century, Pt. I', *Past and Present,* No. 5, pp. 33-53.

—— (1954b) 'The General Crisis of the European Economy in the Seventeenth Century, Pt. II', *Past and Present,* No. 6, pp. 44-65.

—— (1969) *Industry and Empire,* Penguin Books, Harmondsworth.

—— and Rudé, G. (1973) *Captain Swing,* Penguin Books, Harmondsworth.

Holderness, B. A. (1968) *Rural Society in S. E. Lindsey 1660–1840*, PhD thesis, University of Nottingham.

—— (1971) 'Capital Formation in Agriculture', in J. P. P. Higgins and S. Pollard (eds), *Aspects of Capital Investment in Great Britain 1750-1850*, Methuen, London, pp. 159-83.

—— (1972a) 'Landlord's Capital Formation in East Anglia 1750-1870', *Economic History Review,* 2nd series, Vol. 25, pp. 434-47.

—— (1972b) ' "Open" and "Close" Parishes in England in the Eighteenth and Nineteenth Centuries', *Agricultural History Review*, Vol. 20, pp. 126-39.

Hollander, S. (1973) *The Economics of Adam Smith*, Heinemann, London.

Hueckel, G. (1976) 'English Farming Profits during the Napoleonic Wars, 1793-1815', *Explorations in Economic History,* Vol. 13, pp. 331-45.

Hume, D. (1898) *A Treatise of Human Nature*, 2 vols, edited by T. H. Green and T. H. Grose, Longmans, Green and Co., London.

Hunt, H. G. (1957) 'The Chronology of Parliamentary Enclosure in Leicestershire', *Economic History Review,* 2nd series, Vol. 10, pp. 265-72.

—— (1959) 'Landownership and Enclosure 1750-1830', *Economic History Review,* 2nd series, Vol 11, pp. 497-505.

Hussain, A. and Tribe, K. (1981) *Marxism and the Agrarian Question*, 2 vols, Macmillan, London.

Hyams, E. (1971) *Capability Brown and Humphrey Repton,* Dent, London.

John, A. H. (1968) 'The Course of Agricultural Change 1660-1760', in W. E. Minchinton (ed.), *Essays in Agrarian History, Vol. I,* David and Charles, Newton Abbott, pp. 221-53.

Johnson, A. H. (1963) *The Disappearance of the Small Landowner,* Oxford University Press, London.

Johnson, E. A. J. (1937) *Predecessors of Adam Smith,* P. S. King and Son, London.

Jones, E. L. (1962) 'English Farming before and during the Nineteenth Century', *Economic History Review,* 2nd series, Vol. 15, pp. 145-52.

—— (1967) 'Industrial Capital and Landed Investment: The Arkwrights in Herefordshire 1809-43', in E. L. Jones and G. E. Mingay (eds), *Land, Labour and Population in the Industrial Revolution,* Edward Arnold, London, pp. 48-71.

—— (1968) 'Agricultural and Economic Growth in England 1660-1750: Agricultural Change', in W. E. Minchinton (ed.), *Essays in Agrarian History, Vol. I,* David and Charles, Newton Abbott, pp. 203-20.

Joseph, W. (1949) 'The Great English Revolution', *Communist Review,* March, pp. 451-57.

Kent, N. (1775) *Hints to Gentlemen of Landed Property*, J. Dodsley, London.

—— (1976) *General View of the Agriculture of the County of Norfolk,* George Nicol, London.

Kerridge, E. (1967) *The Agricultural Revolution,* George Allen and Unwin, London.

—— (1969) 'The Agricultural Revolution Reconsidered', *Agricultural History,* Vol. 43, pp. 463-75.

Kindleberger, C. (1976) 'The Historical Background: Adam

Smith and the Industrial Revolution', in T. Wilson and A. S. Skinner (eds), *The Market and the State,* Oxford University Press, London, pp. 1-25.

King, G. (1936) 'A Scheme of the Income and Expence of the several families of England Calculated for the Year 1688', in G. E. Barnett (ed.), *Two Tracts by Gregory King,* Johns Hopkins Press, Baltimore.

Kosminsky, E. A. (1928) 'Russian Work on English Economic History', *Economic History Review,* Vol. 1, pp. 208–33.

—— (1955) 'The Evolution of Feudal Rent in England from the XIth. to the XVth. Centuries', *Past and Present,* No. 7, pp. 12–36.

Kuczynski, J. (1940a) 'England's Revolution', *Labour Monthly,* Vol. 22, pp. 558–9.

—— (1940b) 'A Rejoinder', *Labour Monthly,* Vol. 22, pp. 653–5.

Laurence, E. (1727) *The Duty of a Steward to his Lord,* London.

Lavrovsky, V. M. (1937) 'Parliamentary Enclosures in the County of Suffolk (1797–1814)', *Economic History Review,* Vol. 7, pp. 186–208.

Lawrence, J. (1786) *The Modern Land Steward,* 2nd edition, London.

Lazonick, W. (1974) 'Karl Marx and Enclosures in England', *Review of Radical Political Economy,* Vol. 6, No. 2, pp. 1–59.

Le Roy Ladurie, E. (1978) 'A Reply to Professor Brenner', *Past and Present,* No. 79, pp. 55–9.

Lewis, J. (1772) *Uniting and Monopolising Farms, Plainly proved disadvantageous to the Land-Owners, and highly prejudicial to the Public,* 2nd edition, Ipswich.

Linneman, P. (1978) 'An Econometric Examination of the English Parliamentary Enclosure Movement'. *Explorations in Economic History,* Vol. 15, pp.221–8.

Lough, J. (1971) *The 'Encyclopédie',* Longman, London.

Lublinskaya, A. D. (1968) *French Absolutism: The Crucial Phase 1620–1629,* Cambridge University Press, London.

Malcolmson, R. W. (1973) *Popular Recreations in English Society 1700–1850,* Cambridge University Press, London.

Malthus, T. R. (1820) *Principles of Political Economy Considered with a View to their Practical Application,* John Murray, London.

—— (1823) *The Measure of Value Stated and Illustrated,* John Murray, London.

Marshall, W. (1796) *Planting and Rural Ornament*, 2nd edition, G. Nicol, London.
—— (1804) *On the Landed Property of England, an Elementary and Practical Treatise; containing the Purchase, the Improvement, and the Management of Landed Estates,* G. and W. Nicol, London.
—— (1806) *On the Management of Landed Estates: A General Work; for the Use of Professional Men,* Longman, Hurst, Rees, Orme, London.
Martin, J. M. (1966) 'Landownership and the Land Tax Returns', *Agricultural History Review,* Vol. 14, pp. 96–103.
—— (1967) 'The Parliamentary Enclosure Movement and Rural Society in Warwickshire', *Agricultural History Review,* Vol. 15, pp. 19–39.
Marx, K. (1954) *Capital, Vol. 1,* Progress Publishers, Moscow.
—— (1959) *Capital, Vol. 3,* Progress Publishers, Moscow.
—— and Engels, F. (1934) *Selected Correspondence,* Lawrence and Wishart, London.
McCloskey, D. N. (1972) 'The Enclosure of Open Fields: Preface to a Study of its Impact on the Efficiency of English Agriculture in the Eighteenth Century', *Journal of Economic History,* Vol. 32, pp. 15–35.
—— (1975) 'The Economics of Enclosure: A Market Analysis', in E. L. Jones and W. Parker (ed.), *European Peasants and their Markets*, Princeton University Press, Princeton, pp. 123–60.
McCulloch, J. R. (1821) 'The Opinions of Messrs. Say, Sismondi, and Malthus, on Effects of Machinery and Accumulation', *Edinburgh Review,* Vol. 35, March, pp. 102–23.
McGregor, O. R. (1961) 'Research Possibilities for Family Study', *British Journal of Sociology,* Vol. 12, pp. 310–17.
McKendrick, N. (1970) 'Josiah Wedgwood and Cost Accounting in the Industrial Revolution', *Economic History Review,* 2nd series, Vol. 23, pp. 45–67.
Meek, R. L. (1976) *Social Science and the Ignoble Savage,* Cambridge University Press, London.
Mercer, W. B. (1939) 'William Tompson: A Record of Georgian Farming', *Journal of the Ministry of Agriculture,* Vol. 45, pp. 1125–32.
Mingay, G. E. (1962) 'The Size of Farms in the Eighteenth Century', *Economic History Review*, 2nd series, Vol. 14, pp. 469–88.

—— (1963) *English Landed Society in the Eighteenth Century*, Routledge and Kegan Paul, London.
—— (1964) 'The Land Tax Assessment and the Small Landowner', *Economic History Review,* 2nd series, Vol. 17, pp. 381-8.
—— (1968) *Enclosure and the Small Farmer in the Age of the Industrial Revolution,* Macmillan, London.
—— 'Dr Kerridge's "Agricultural Revolution": A comment', *Agricultural History*, Vol. 43, pp. 447-81.
Mordant, J. (1761) *The Complete Steward: or, the Duty of a Steward to his Lord,* 2 vols, London.
Müller-Mertens, E. (1977) 'Skizze zur weiteren Verständingung über das feudale Produktionsverhältnis', in L. Kuchenbuch and B. Michael (eds), *Feudalismus – Materialen zur Theorie und Geschichte,* Verlag Ullstein, Frankfurt, pp. 349-83.
Napoleoni, C. (1975) *Smith Ricardo Marx,* Basil Blackwell, Oxford.
Nef, J. (1943) 'The Industrial Revolution Reconsidered', *Journal of Economic History,* Vol. 3, pp. 1-31.
Orwin, C. S. (1938) 'The History of Tenant Right', *Agricultural Progress,* Vol. 15, pp. 147-51.
Orwin, C. S. and C. S. (1967) *The Open Fields*, 3rd edition, Oxford University Press, London.
Oschinsky, D. (1971) *Walter of Henley and Other Treatises on Estate Management and Accounting,* Oxford University Press, London.
Parker, L. A. (1949) 'The Agrarian Revolution at Cotesback 1501-1612', in W. G. Hoskins (ed.), *Studies in Leicestershire Agrarian History,* Leicestershire Archaeological Society, pp. 41-76.
Parker, R. A. C. (1955) 'Coke of Norfolk and the Agricultural Revolution', *Economic History Review,* 2nd series, Vol. 8, pp. 156-66.
—— (1975) *Coke of Norfolk. A Financial and Agricultural Study 1707-1842,* Oxford University Press, London.
Philpot, G. (1975) 'Enclosure and Population Growth in Eighteenth Century England', *Explorations in Economic History,* Vol. 12, pp. 29-46.
Pollard, S. (1965) *The Genesis of Modern Management*, Edward Arnold, London.
—— (1968) 'The Growth and Distribution of Capital in Great

Britain, c. 1770–1870', *Third International Conference of Economic History,* Vol. I, Mouton, Paris, pp. 335–65.

Postan, M. M. (1936) Review of Kosminsky, *The English Village in the Thirteenth Century* (Leningrad 1935), *Economic History Review,* Vol. 6, pp. 223–6.

— and Hatcher, J. (1978) 'Population and Class Relations in Feudal Society', *Past and Present*, No. 78, pp. 24–37.

Rapp, D. (1974) 'Social Mobility in the Eighteenth Century: The Whitbreads of Bedfordshire, 1720–1815', *Economic History Review,* 2nd series, Vol. 27, pp. 380–94.

Ravensdale, J. R. (1974) *Liable to Floods – Village Landscape on the Edge of the Fens AD450–1850,* Cambridge University Press, London.

Ricardo, D. (1951–2) *Works and Correspondence,* edited by P. Sraffa and M. H. Dobb, Vols I–IX, Cambridge University Press, London.

Richards, E. (1973) *The Leviathan of Wealth,* Routledge and Kegan Paul, London.

Riches, N. (1937) *The Agricultural Revolution in Norfolk,* University of North Carolina Press, Chapel Hill.

Robertson, T. (1796) *Outline of the General Report on the Size of Farms*, Edinburgh.

Rogers, J. E. T. (1866–1902) *A History of Agriculture and Prices in England,* 7 vols, Macmillan, London.

Roll, E. (1954) *A History of Economic Thought,* 3rd edition, Faber and Faber, London.

Rose, R. B. (1961) 'Eighteenth Century Price Riots and Public Policy in England', *International Review of Social History,* Vol. 6, pp. 277–92.

Saville, J. (1969) 'Primitive Accumulation and Early Industrialisation in Britain', *Socialist Register 1969,* pp. 247–71.

Schumpeter, J. A. (1954a) *History of Economic Analysis,* Oxford University Press, New York.

— (1954b) *Economic Doctrine and Method*, George Allen and Unwin, London.

Scott, W. R. (1937) *Adam Smith as Student and Professor,* Jackson, Son and Co., Glasgow.

Shelton, W. J. (1973) *English Hunger and Industrial Disorders,* Macmillan, London.

Skocpol, T. (1977) 'Wallerstein's World Capitalist System: A Theoretical and Historical Critique', *American Journal of Sociology,* Vol. 82, pp. 1075–90.

—— and Fulbrook, M. (1977) Review of Anderson, *Passages* and *Lineages, Journal of Development Studies,* Vol. 13, 290–5.

Slater, G. (1907) *The English Peasantry and the Enclosure of Common Fields,* Archibald Constable and Co., London.

Slicher van Bath, B. H. (1963) *The Agrarian History of Western Europe 500–1850*, Edward Arnold, London.

Smith, A. (1970) *The Wealth of Nations,* Penguin Books, Harmondsworth.

—— (1976a) *An Inquiry into the Nature and Causes of the Wealth of Nations,* 2 vols. Oxford University Press, Oxford.

—— (1976b) *The Theory of Moral Sentiments,* Oxford University Press, Oxford.

—— (1978) *Lectures on Jurisprudence,* Oxford University Press, Oxford.

Spufford, M. (1974) *Contrasting Communities,* Cambridge University Press, London.

Squarey, E. P. (1878) 'Farm Capital', *Journal of the Royal Agricultural Society of England,* 2nd series, Vol. 14, pp. 427–44.

Stevenson, J. (1974) 'Food Riots in England, 1792–1818', in R. Quinault and J. Stevenson, *Popular Protest and Public Order,* George Allen and Unwin, London, pp. 33–74.

Steuart, J. (1966) *An Inquiry into the Principles of Political Oeconomy,* 2 vols, Oliver and Boyd, Edinburgh.

Stewart, D. (1811) *Biographical Memoirs of Adam Smith, LLD, of William Robertson, DD and of Thomas Reid, DD*. Edinburgh.

Sturgess, R. W. (1966) 'The Agricultural Revolution on the on the English Clays', *Agricultural History Review,* Vol. 14, pp. 104–21.

Sweezy, P. (1976a) 'A Critique', in R. Hilton (ed.), *The Transition from Feudalism to Capitalism,* NLB, London, pp. 33–56.

—— (1976b) 'A Rejoinder', in R. Hilton (ed.), *The Transition from Feudalism to Capitalism,* NLB, London, pp. 102–8.

Takahashi, K. (1976) 'A Contribution to the Discussion', in R. Hilton (ed.), *The Transition from Feudalism to Capitalism,* NLB, London, pp. 68–97.

Tann, J. (1970) *The Development of the Factory,* Cornmarket Press, London.

Tawney, R. H. (1912) *The Agrarian Problem in the Sixteenth Century*, Longmans, Green and Co, London.

—— (1978) 'A History of Capitalism', in *History and Society*, Routledge and Kegan Paul, London, pp. 202–14.

Taylor, C. (1973) *The Cambridgeshire Landscape,* Hodder and Stoughton, London.

Taylor, W. L. (1965) *Francis Hutcheson and David Hume as Predecessors of Adam Smith*, Duke University Press, Dur-Ham (N. Carolina).

Thirsk, J. (1959) *Tudor Enclosures,* Historical Association.

—— (1964) 'The Common Fields', *Past and Present*, No. 29, pp. 3–25.

—— (1967) 'Enclosing and Engrossing', in J. Thirsk (ed.), *The Agrarian History of England and Wales. Vol. IV 1500–1640,* Cambidge University Press, London, pp. 200–55.

Thomas, D. (1972) 'The Social Origins of Marriage Partners of the British Peerage in the Eighteenth and Nineteenth Centuries', *Population Studies,* Vol. 26, pp. 99–111.

Thomas, J. (1971) *The Rise of the Staffordshire Potteries,* Adams and Dart, Bath.

Thompson, E. P. (1965) 'The Peculiarities of the English', in *Socialist Register 1965,* pp. 311–62.

—— (1968) *The Making of the English Working Class,* Penguin Books, Harmondsworth.

—— (1971) 'The Moral Economy of the English Crowd in the Eighteenth Century', *Past and Present,* No. 50, pp. 76–136.

Thompson, F. M. L. (1963) *English Landed Society in the Nineteenth Century,* Routledge and Kegan Paul, London.

—— (1968) 'The Second Agricultural Revolution 1815–80', *Economic History Review*, 2nd series, Vol. 21, pp. 62–77.

—— (1969) 'Landownership and Economic Growth in England in the Eighteenth Century', in E. L. Jones and S. J. Woolf (eds), *Agrarian Change and Economic Development,* Methuen, London, pp. 41–60.

Thompson, R. J. (1907) 'An Inquiry into the Rent of Agricultural Land in England and Wales during the Nineteenth Century', *Journal of the Royal Statistical Society,* Vol. 70, pp. 587–625.

Timmer, C. P. (1969) 'The Turnip, the New Husbandry, and the English Agricultural Revolution', *Quarterly Journal of Economics,* Vol. 83, pp. 375–95.

Titow, J. Z. (1965) 'Medieval England and the Open-Field System', *Past and Present* No. 32, pp. 86–102.

Torr, D. (1941) 'The English Revolution', *Labour Monthly,* February, pp. 90-2.

Toynbee, A. (1890) *Lectures on the Industrial Revolution of the 18th. Century in England,* 3rd edition, Longmans, Green and Co, London.

Tribe, K. (1978) *Land, Labour and Economic Discourse,* Routledge and Kegan Paul, London.

—— (1975) 'Capitalism and Industrialisation', in *Intervention* No. 5, pp. 23-37.

von Tunzelman, G. N. (1978) *Steam Power and British Industrialisation to 1860,* Oxford University Press, Oxford.

Ure, A. (1835) *The Philosophy of Manufactures,* Charles Knight, London.

Wädekin, K.-E. (ed.) (1952) *Zur Periodisierung des Feudalismus und Kapitalismus in der geschichtlichen Entwicklung der UdSSR,* Verlag Kultur und Fortschritt, Berlin.

Wallerstein, I. (1974) *The Modern World System,* Academic Press, London.

Ward, J. R. (1974) *The Finance of Canal Building in Eighteenth Century England,* Oxford University Press, London.

Willan, T. S. (1936) *River Navigation in England 1600-1750,* Oxford University Press, London.

—— (1938) *The English Coasting Trade 1600-1750*, Manchester University Press, Manchester.

Wimpey, J. (1772) *An Essay on the Present high Price of Provisions,* T. Davies, London.

Wordie, J. R. (1967) *A Great Landed Estate in the Eighteenth Century – Aspects of Management on the Leveson-Gower Properties, 1691-1833,* PhD thesis, University of Reading.

—— (1974) 'Social Change on the Leveson-Gower Estates, 1714-1832', *Economic History Review,* 2nd series, Vol. 27, pp. 593-609.

Wunder, H. (1978) 'Peasant Organisation and Class Conflict in East and West Germany', *Past and Present*, No. 78, pp; 47-55.

Yamey, B. S. (1964) 'Accounting and the Rise of Capitalism: Further Notes on a Theme by Sombart', *Journal of Accounting Research,* Vol. 2, pp. 117-36.

Young, A. (1770a) *The Farmer's Guide in Hiring and Stocking Farms*, 2 vols, W. Strahan and W. Nicoll, London.

—— (1770b) *A Course of Experimental Husbandry*, 2 vols, J. Dodsley, London.

—— (1770c) *Rural Oeconomy*, T. Becket, London.
—— (1771) *The Farmer's Kalendar*, Robinson and Roberts, London.

Index